THE

PSALMS

OF THE

FIRST COVENANT PEOPLE OF GOD

THE
PSALMS
OF THE
FIRST COVENANT PEOPLE OF GOD

MATHEW V. THEKKEKARA SDB

iUniverse, Inc.
Bloomington

The Psalms of the First Covenant People of God

The scriptural quotations in the book are from the New Revised Standard Version of the Bible: Catholic Edition. Copyright 1993 and 1989. Printed at Theological Publications of India (TPI) under authorisation of Thomas Nelson, Inc.

iUniverse books may be ordered through booksellers or by contacting:

iUniverse
1663 Liberty Drive
Bloomington, IN 47403
www.iuniverse.com
1-800-Authors (1-800-288-4677)

ISBN: 978-1-4759-8185-8 (sc)
ISBN: 978-1-4759-8186-5 (ebk)

Library of Congress Control Number: 2013905096

Printed in the United States of America

iUniverse rev. date: 03/27/2013

To my mother, Mariam Varkey Thekkekara,
who celebrated her ninety-fifth birthday on November 12, 2012

FOREWORD

I t is my distinct privilege to comment on Father Mathew's scholarly and perceptive study on the Book of Psalms. It is a work of love before being a work of scholarship, intended primarily for students in a theological seminary but one that would benefit a far wider Christian readership. Any person desirous of being introduced to a classic source of Christian prayer and spirituality would find a sure guide in Father Mathew's work.

Part I presents a preliminary approach to the psalms, in which Father Mathew deals succinctly with the psalms as a "school of prayer," but he readily admits that praying with the psalms has its difficulties. These arise largely from the fact that the psalms reflect different religious and cultural backgrounds, different liturgical and prayer forms, different literary and poetic styles, and different conceptions of the world and of our place in it.

A scientific, exegetical study of the psalms at these different levels provides a basis for a Christian understanding of the psalms. A Christian interpretation sees Christ and the New Testament as the fulfillment of all the promises of the Old Testament. In this understanding, the Psalter is seen as a Christian Bible in miniature.

Part II contains a sizable introduction to the Book of Psalms, beginning with the title and numbering, followed by (a) formation of the Psalter (compilation, early collections, five books), date (of individual psalms/collections), and titles (authorship designations and other devices), and (b) Hebrew poetry: notably, parallelism and its forms, meter, and other poetic features.

Part II also deals with the life setting (*Sitz im Leben*) of the psalms with reference to ancient Israeli cultic festivals. This section briefly describes theories put forward by such scholars as Hermann Gunkel, Sigmund Mowinckel, Artur Weiser, and Hans-Joachim Kraus.

Part II concludes with extensive paragraphs about the theology of the psalms and the New Testament.

Part III begins by discussing approaches to psalm study and their classification, based on the work of these biblical scholars: A. F. Kirkpatrick, Charles Augustus Briggs, Moses Buttenwieser, Herman Gunkel, Sigmund Mowinckel, Artur Weiser, Hans-Joachim Kraus, and Claus Westermann.

On this basis, Father Mathew proceeds to list the 150 psalms of the Psalter, indicating the form to which each belongs. This is followed by a list of twelve literary forms, followed by which psalms belong to each form.

These lists conclude the introductory section, which is followed by the commentary proper.

One can only be amazed at the breadth of the research involved, of the scholarship of the presentation, and above all by the author's love for the word of God.

Father Arthur J. Lenti, SDB, MA, SSL

CONTENTS

PREFACE

The current Year of Faith (October 11, 2012 to November 24, 2013) commemorates the fiftieth anniversary of the opening of the Second Vatican Council and the twentieth anniversary of the publication of the Catechism of the Catholic Church. We shall try at this moment to pay special attention to the Second Vatican Council.

The function of the revision of the Divine Office was "to nourish the spiritual life of the people of God"[1] (clergy and laity alike). The purpose was to rediscover and promote the regular tradition of daily community prayer, a practice carried on by the early church, making morning and evening prayers accessible to all members of the community of the people of God. Vatican II described morning and evening prayers as "the two hinges on which the Daily Office turns."[2]

This book can be viewed as emerging from this trend. This book is directed to theologate seminarians, priests, and learned readers. The study of the psalms need not be stopped here. My next book, *The Psalms for the Second Covenant People of God*, is meant for all Christians, the second covenant people of God. Our acquaintance with the psalms should not stop with just studying them. The psalms are prayers. Hence the title of another of my books: *The People of God in Faith Praying the Psalms Meaningfully*.

---

[1]   *Laudis Canticum,* 8 (a constitution promulgating the Divine Office).

[2]   *Sacrosanctum Concilium,* 89 (the constitution of liturgy).

This book examines the psalms of Israel, the first covenant people of God. It is the fruit of my years of teaching psalms to seminarians. My students brought up to me a number of questions and doubts about the different aspects of the psalms. Their interest and readiness to learn more about the psalms encouraged me to write this book. Many Christians are eager to scientifically analyse the different aspects of the psalms. These kinds of Christians can employ this book as a guide in their search for more knowledge of the psalms.

In the seminary, this book can be employed as a basic study tool. It book can fill in the vacuum, if one exists, of textbooks on the psalms. Priests can use this book in their ministry. Educated readers can employ this book for a serious study of the psalms.

The Psalms of the First Covenant People of God does not claim to be the last word on the psalms. It may be seen as a signboard directing readers to the huge wealth held within the psalms. Putting it in another way, the book can be compared to a rudimentary capsule that can make us taste the psalms. My prayers is that we, the Second Covenant people of God, are carried back in prayer through the psalms to a closer personal relationship with our God.

The Psalms of the First Covenant People of God does not discuss all the psalms, but this book may be considered a pioneering effort that can lead readers in their search for greater knowledge of the psalms and as an aid for those who are diving into their depths.

My sincere thanks go to Mr. P. V. Mathew, who went through the initial text of the book and made valuable suggestions. May he make ever greater progress in all his other endeavours. A computer technician, Mr. Mike Stromitis, guided me to computerise my book. All the best to him in all his activities. Mr. Sean Roche, another computer expert, guided me in the arrangement of my book. My sincere words of gratitude flow to him. Sincere thanks to all my students, who share in my work. If there are any shortcomings in the book, they fall on me.

My book is dedicated to my mother, Mariam Varkey Thekkekara, who celebrated her ninety-fifth birthday on November 12, 2012.

Mathew Thekkekara
Institute of Salesian Studies
Berkeley, CA

ABBREVIATIONS

AB	Anchor Bible
AD	*Anno Domini*
ATC	Asian Trading Corporation
BC	Before Christ
BT	*Bible Today*
CBQ	*Catholic Biblical Quarterly*
CE	Common Era
EDB	*Exegetical Dictionary of the Bible*
IDB	*Interpreter's Dictionary of the Bible*
IDB Sup	*Interpreter's Dictionary of the Bible Supplement*
JBC	*Jerome Biblical Commentary*
LXX	Septuagint
MT	Masoretic Text
NAB	New American Bible
NEB	New English Bible
NIB	New Interpreter's Bible
NJB	New Jerusalem Bible
NJBC	*New Jerome Biblical Commentary*
NRSV	New Revised Standard Version
NT	New Testament
OT	Old Testament
OTL	Old Testament Library
Ps.	Psalm
RSV	Revised Standard Version
RB	*Revue Biblique*
TPI	Theological Publications of India
TD	*Theology Digest*
YHWH	Yahweh

AN INTRODUCTION TO
PRAYING THE PSALMS

Desire to pray comes from a deep-rooted desire to love and know God. This yearning comes as a response to God's love. Those in love spend time together. We want to spend time in communion with God; we want to pray the psalms. But we need help in learning to pray, and *The Young in Faith Praying the Psalms Meaningfully*[3] can give us the help we need. The psalms express a whole range of human emotions in prayer, and praying the psalms gives voice to the deepest movements of the soul.

As children learn to write, we learn to pray. The Holy Spirit is our teacher. We learn to pray by taking the prayers inspired by the Holy Spirit and copying them, following the movement of the Spirit with mind and heart. This is the fundamental principle presupposed in *The Young in Faith Praying the Psalms Meaningfully.*

[3]   Mathew V. Thekkekara, *The Young in Faith Praying the Psalms Meaningfully* (Bangalore: ATC, 2005).

That book provides a pattern of prayer rooted in the scriptures, in the experience of Jesus, and in the life of his church. It is a way that has enriched the faith experience of countless Christians.

The Book of Psalms is a mini-Bible or, to use the words of Martin Luther, the whole Gospel in a nutshell.[4] It is the prayer book of the Bible, the prayer book par excellence. The Book of Psalms is also a school of prayer (see the next page). A psalm is "a song sung to the accompaniment of musical instruments." The Book of Psalms, also called the "Psalter," is a perfect form of prayer for all. The psalms we possess were composed over a period of six hundred to seven hundred years (from 1000 BCE to 300 BCE). Traditionally they are called the "Psalms of David," who might have contributed something to their composition. But it is more accurate to say that the psalms were written by many unnamed persons. In the third century BCE, the Psalter was finally compiled in the form that we see today.

1. The Lay People Praying the Psalms

In the early church, the psalms were the prayers of the whole Christian community. By the end of the second century, the principal times of prayer were at daybreak and at sunset (morning and evening prayers). These two hours of prayer were assumed to be obligatory for all Christians. They were encouraged to meet together to pray; if not, to pray alone. In the early centuries of the church, Christians in all the different countries included morning and evening prayer as part of the cycle of prayer. That the clergy and laity were encouraged to attend daily morning and evening prayers is noted in the document *Apostolic Constitutions* (c. AD 380).

---

[4]   John F. Craghan, *Psalms for All Seasons* (Bangalore: IJA Publication, 1996), 3.

In subsequent centuries, monastic influence in praying the psalms became stronger and stronger, with a corresponding decline in the participation of the laity. By the twelfth century, praying the psalms in the Western church had become by and large private prayer, read in Latin from the Breviary, confined basically to priests and religious. The communal character of the prayer of the psalms was preserved chiefly in the monasteries. This is far from what the times of prayer were intended to be for all in the beginning of the church.

The essential purpose of praying the psalms, after the Vatican II revision of the Divine Office, was "to nourish the spiritual life of the people of God" (*Laudis Canticum*, 8), i.e., clergy and laity alike. The inspiration for the reform of Vatican II was the example of the early church, where morning and evening prayers were observed by all the people of God. The purpose of the reform was to rediscover the essential traditions of daily prayer as practiced in the early church, making morning and evening prayer accessible to all Christians. Vatican II describes morning and evening prayer as "the two hinges on which the daily office turns" (*Sacrosanctum Concilium*, 89).[5]

2. Praying the Psalms

The Book of Psalms is a school of prayer. The psalms will help us to rise with mind, heart, and body through prayer into the realm of God. The ancient meetings with God's word and deed are the psalms, prayer records of faith in every situation of life and death. The psalms are authentic and solid spirituality. "If we keep vigil in the church," says St. John Chrysostom, "David[6]

---

[5]   See John Brook, *The School of Prayer. An Introduction to the Divine Office for All Christians* (London: Harper Collins, 1992), 1-8.

[6]   Traditionally, all the palms are attributed to David.

comes first, last, and midst. If early in the morning we seek for the melody of hymns, first, last, and midst is David again. If we are occupied with the funeral solemnities of the departed, if virgins sit at home and spin, David is first, last, and midst."[7] St. Jeremy echoes in a similar vein: "The labourer, while he holds the handle of the plough, sings Alleluia; the tired reaper employs himself in the psalms; and the vine dresser, while lopping the vines with his curved hook, sings something of David. These are our ballads in this part of the world: these (to use the common expression) are our love-songs."[8]

The above practice of the church praying the psalms was in perfect harmony with the Israelite tradition of prayer. Individuals in the Bible transformed into prayer all the realities that crowded their lives. In the Book of Psalms, we can see from time to time all the chords of the human heart vibrate, from the exultation of the one who sings, "I will praise the Lord as long as I live; I will sing praises to my God all my life long" (Ps. 146:2) to the agony of the one who cries out, "For we sink down to the dust; our bodies cling to the ground" (Ps. 44:25) and invokes God's help. Having contemplated nature with an eye full of admiration and awe, the psalmist sees in it the God of glory: "In his temple all say 'Glory'" (Ps. 29:9). It is nothing other than the temple of the universe (cf. Ps. 104:24).

With his mind's eye, the poet turns the events of the history of salvation over and over and recognises them as God's marvels or mighty deeds (*magnalia Dei*). They are, for him, the signs of salvation from a God who is ever faithful (*emet*), and his steadfast love (*hesed*) becomes the key to interpreting everything: "His steadfast love endures for ever" (Ps. 136).

---

[7] J. M. Neale and R. F. Littledale, *A Commentary on the Psalms: From Primitive and Medieval Writers* (London: Joseph Masters, 1976), 1.
[8] Ibid., 5.

Not only the beauty of nature and the great history of salvation become prayer in the psalms but also the simple story of each one with the humdrum events of daily life: the joy of the intimacy created by the family (Ps. 128:3), the hurt caused by the betrayal of a friend (Ps. 41:9), the atmosphere of mirth that takes all by contagion when they gather in the fruits of the earth (Ps. 126:5-6), and so on. Every human experience is enclosed in the psalms. In fact, it is "one of the few books in which one is completely at home, however preoccupied and unsettled and troubled one may be."[9]

3. Difficulties in Praying the Psalms

To many Christians, the Book of Psalms is an uncelebrated and "closed book." Its obscurity may be due to the following factors:

i.   We have never seen our parents praying the psalms. As a consequence, we may not have acquired the habit of using these beautiful poems as personal prayers.

ii. There is a lack of in-depth study of the psalms. As a result the imagery in them has remained remote (Ps. 98:8, 29:5-6, 133:2) and their poetry unfamiliar.[10]

iii. A lack of harmony between our Christian soul and the soul of the psalmist. This is expressed in our feeling a) that we have attained a moral level different from that which is referred to in the psalms (unkindness, vengefulness, imprecations in them), b) that we have reached a level where we understand peace, blessing,

---

[9]   G. von Rad, *Old Testament Theology* (London: SCM, 1965), 399.

[10]   K. Luke, *Taste and See. Aids to the Fruitful Recitation of the Breviary* (Cochin: Impress, 1980), iii.

life, and salvation with relation to God other than that of the psalms, which tie us down to earth, and c) that their history is past and gone (Abraham, Moses, Samuel, David, the exile, the return of the temple, and its feasts).[11]

The psalms are the expressions of the piety of the Old Testament people, and they have to become contemporary to the people of God today and expressions of our own piety.

4. We, Christians, Pray the Psalms

The psalms are the expressions of the piety of the Old Testament people, and they have to become contemporary to us, the people of God today, as expressions of our own piety. Thomas Merton speaks of three different types of people who pray the psalms: The first group admits that the psalms are a perfect form of prayer, but they are unable to use them in their own prayer and never, in fact, do so. They pray the psalms without much appreciation or understanding. The second group has a strong conviction of the value of the psalms, a conviction that is a moving force in their lives. But it still does not permit them to enter into the psalms. This is the case of some monks and clerics who are loyal to the supremacy of vocal prayer and convinced that they are doing a very important thing. Their zeal for the psalms remains largely material and exterior. They do not know the meaning of the psalms and do not really care to know either. Their business is to recite them with meticulous care. The third group knows by experience that the psalms are a perfect prayer, a prayer in which Christ prays in the Christian soul. They have entered into the psalms with faith. They have in a sense "lived"

---

[11]   See Albert Gelin, *The Psalms Are Our Prayers* (Collegeville, MN: The Liturgical Press, 1964), 51-52.

out the meaning of some of the psalms in their own lives. They have tasted and seen that the Lord is sweet.[12] We have to learn to pray by praying.

i. Making the Psalms Our Own (Appropriation)

The realities in the life of Israel that became prayer for her needs are not always the realities that we live. Through the psalms, we too have to speak to make them our prayer. That is making them our own. If they merely contain the experiences of another people, they can only satisfy our curiosity. Their experiences and expressions must become our experiences and expressions of our desires, feelings, and so on. Otherwise there is no prayer. Such transference can take place when we try to make them our own.

a. Making the Psalms Our Own (Appropriation) at the Human Level

One can make another's experience one's own in two ways: at the same level (flood, drought), and at the sympathetic level (taking the place of another), like an actor on the stage, or like one who takes things from others and makes them their own (one in love). The person who prays the psalms has to be not like the actor but like one in love. If one does not feel anything about the psalms, then they do not become prayer.

---

[12] See Thomas Merton, *Praying the Psalms* (Collegeville, MN: Liturgical Press, 1956), 20-21.

b. Making the Psalms Our Own (Appropriation) at the Christian Level

Making the psalms our own at the Christian level is possible i) at the personal level. The psalms touch upon various emotions. These emotions are personal and general. "What is most personal is most general" (Carl Rogers). ii) It also takes place at the Christian traditional level. The New Testament tradition has nothing similar to the psalms, as the other parts of the OT do: The Pentateuch = the Gospels; the Prophets = the Epistles; wisdom literature = James and Peter. It means that the New Testament community accepted the psalms as they were and used them as such.[13] In the early centuries, the Book of Psalms was the church's one prayer book for both clergy and laity (1 Cor. 14:26, Eph. 5:19, Col. 3:16-17).

c. Making the Psalms Our Own (Appropriation) at the Spiritual Level

Our Christian instinct teaches us that it is the Spirit who makes us cry, "*Abba* [Father]." The same Spirit inspired the writing of the psalms. If we let ourselves be led by the Spirit, he will make us enter into the psalms.

ii. Christ, the Key to the Book of Psalms

The Book of Psalms is a closed book. To the fathers of the church, Christ is the master key to the Book of Psalms (cf. Lk. 24:44). The theological basis of our endeavour to actualise the psalms is the fact of the promise of salvation and fulfillment

---

[13] See Francis Martin, *Songs of God's People: The Psalms as Poetry and Prayer* (Denville, NJ: Dimension Books, 1978), 16.

in Christ. As a result, Christ now stands as the bond of union between the two testaments. The Christian community's actualisation of the psalms is necessarily Christ centered.[14] He becomes the key to our understanding of the psalms. He is at once the singer of the psalms and their hero.

a. Christ, the Singer of the Psalms

The Jewish practice of daily prayer was the school in which Jesus learnt to pray. He prayed, like every Jew, three times a day: morning prayer at sunrise, afternoon prayer at the time of the sacrifice in the temple of Jerusalem (c. 3:00 p.m.), and evening prayer at nightfall. These three "hours" of prayer were the daily habit of every devout Jew.[15]

At the age of twelve, the religious adulthood, Jesus went up to Jerusalem, and he would have sung the psalms of ascent (Ps. 120-134) with the other pilgrims. Each year at Passover, he would have joined in the Great Hallel (praise) (Ps. 136), which tells of God's glorious deeds in rescuing his people from Egypt. After the Last Supper, he would have sung the Egyptian Hallel (Ps. 113-118), which was the traditional conclusion to the Passover meal. In the agony of dying, it was to the psalms that he turned: "My God, my God, why have you forsaken me?" (Ps. 22:1). His final words on the cross are, "Father, into your hands I commend my Spirit" (Ps. 31:5).[16]

Jesus, "this marvelous singer of the psalms" (St. Augustine), prayed the psalms. The psalms were prayers of Christ. We pray

---

14 Luke, *Taste*, xii.
15 See Brook, *School of Prayer*, 6.
16 Richard Atherton, *New Light* (Mumbai: Pauline Publications, 1996), 16.

them with and through Christ. "As God he is prayed to; as man he prays" (St. Augustine).[17]

b. Christ, the Hero of the Psalms

i) The Book of Psalms becomes the Prayer Book of the church, a prayer book "full of the incarnate word." The psalms speak of Christ, are most intelligible in terms of Christ, and attain their deepest meaning only in Christ.[18] In the New Testament, there are ninety-three quotations from more than sixty psalms. The New Testament found Jesus' whole life sketched out in the psalms: Ps. 69:9 = Jn 2:17; Ps. 22:7 = Mt. 27:39, Mk 15:29, Lk. 23:35; Ps. 22:18 = Mt. 27:35, Mk 15:24, Lk. 23:34, Jn 19:24; Ps. 16:10 = Acts 2:27.

ii) The psalms can be looked at as being addressed to Christ. What was spoken of Yahweh in the psalms can be transferred to Christ: Ps. 8:2 = Mt. 21:16; Ps. 118:26 = Mt. 23:37-39; Ps. 82:6 = Jn 10:34; Ps. 118:22-23 = Mk 12:10-11; Ps. 102:25-27 = Heb. 1:10-12; Ps. 7:9 = Rev. 2:23; Ps. 68:18 = Eph. 4:8; Ps. 34:8 = 1 Pet. 2:3.[19]

In his intimacy with God and his habit of spending hours alone with his Father, Jesus went far beyond the traditional Jewish practices of prayer. These, however, laid the foundation for his unique prayer relationship with his Father.

The Gospels show us Jesus praying at the critical moments of his life: at baptism; on the night before he chose his apostles;

---

17   See Gelin, *Psalms*, 52-57.
18   See Eugene S. Geissler, ed., *The Bible Prayer Book* (Notre Dame, IN: Ave Maria Press, 1981), 232.
19   See Gelin, *Psalms*, 57-61.

before he healed the deaf man; when he taught his disciples to pray; when they returned after their first mission; on the night before his passion; at the Last Supper; and on the Cross. Prayer animated his whole ministry.[20]

5. Christ and the Church

Praying the psalms means going beyond the literal sense to the fuller meaning intended by God for Christ and his church. The psalms speak of the church's relationship to God. The mystery of God's self-revelation and self-gift to Israel in the Old Testament prefigured what was to be accomplished in Christ and in the church. God has given himself totally to humans in Christ. God's union with the people in the Old Testament looks forward to Christ's union with the church. In saying the psalms, which recount God's love for Israel, the church is speaking of her union with Jesus Christ.

---

[20]   See Brook, *School of Prayer*, 7-8.

AN INTRODUCTION
TO THE PSALMS

T he Masoretic Text (MT), the Hebrew Bible, was divided into three sections: the Law (*Torah*), the Prophets (*Nebi'im*), and the Writings (*Kethubim*). The Book of Psalms, *Sepher Tehillim* (Book of Songs), is the first book in the Writings section.[21] The psalms have a double identity. They are scripture and liturgy. They are found as a book in the Bible and found in our church songs, lectionaries, and prayer. They are also the liturgical poetry of ancient Israel. First of all, we can look at the Psalter as a "song book," but that fails to take account of the large number of prayer texts it contains. In addition to this fact, the Psalter presents itself as a body of texts (wisdom psalms) useful for "meditation and reflection" (Ps. 1:1), for governing life and human action. Hence we must admit that the Psalter incorporates prayer, hymnody, and meditative reflection.[22]

Athanasius of Alexandria, in his letter to Marcellinus, lays down four ideas about the psalms:

21 Peter C. Craigie, *Psalms 1-50. Word Biblical Commentary*, 19 (Waco, TX: Word Books, 1983), 42.
22 J. David Pleins, *The Psalms. Songs of Tragedy, Hope, and Justice* (Maryknoll, NY: Orbis Books, 1993), 3.

1. The Psalter is a Bible in miniature. In it, those who believe in Christ find the essentials of all that is found in the Bible as a whole.
2. People can be utterly at home in the Psalter. There they find expression for all types of human experience.
3. The Psalter is used by all who believe in Christ. Thus those who pray the psalms do so in the community of the saints.
4. The Psalter is a pure mirror of Christianity. It leads us to self-recognition, to God, and to all creatures.[23]

Here we can note what Luther said in his *Preface to the Psalms*: "Here we find not only what one or two saints have done, but what he has done who is the very head of all the saints. We also find what all the saints still do . . . . The Psalter ought to be a precious and beloved book, if for no other reason than this: it promises Christ's death and resurrection so clearly—and pictures his kingdom and the condition and nature of all Christendom—that it might well be called a little Bible."[24] The prayer of Christ the Head carries the prayer of the church yesterday and today. This fact implies that Christ has become the one who was really praying in the psalms.

1. The Title

In the Masoretic Text, the psalms are entitled *tehillim*: "praise" or "songs of praise" or "hymns." Strangely enough, *tehillim* has a masculine form, while in the singular it is feminine. Probably the compilers meant it to denote the song book as a whole. The word "psalm" is a transliteration, via Latin (*psalmus*), of the Greek

---

[23] Hans Winfried Juengling, "Psalms 1-41," in *The International Bible Commentary. An Ecumenical Commentary for the Twenty-First Century,* ed. William R. Farmer (Bangalore: TPI, 2004), 836-837.
[24] Hans-Joachim Kraus, *Theology of the Psalms,* trans. Keith Crim (Minneapolis: Augsburg Publishing House, 1986), 13.

psalmos, which is a translation of the Hebrew *mizmor* (the title of fifty-seven psalms): "a song sung to the accompaniment of musical instruments." The name "psalms" derives from the Greek *psalmoi,* songs of praise. The *Codex Vaticanus* (AD fourth century) of the LXX has the title *psalmoi* ("psalms") and the subtitle *biblos psalmon* ("Book of Psalms").[25] The word "psalms" occurs also in the NT (Lk. 20:42, 24:44; Acts 1:20). *Codex Alexandrinus* of the LXX calls the collection of 150 psalms *psalterion* ("a stringed instrument"). From it springs the traditional name "Psalter" (the Book of Psalms).

2. Numbering of the Psalms

The MT has 150 psalms, and the Septuagint (LXX) has 151 psalms, of which the last is noncanonical.

MT (NRSV, NJB, NEB, NAB)[26]	LXX (Vulgate, Breviary)
1-8	1-8
9-10	9a, 9b
11-113	10-112
114-115	113a, 113b
116:1-9	114
116:10-19	115
117-146	116-145
147:1-11	146
147:12-20	147
148-150	148-150[27]

---

25   James L. Crenshaw, *The Psalms. An Introduction* (Grand Rapids, MI: Eerdmans, 2001), 3.

26   Craigie, *Psalms,* 2, 42.

27   Hebrew numbering is usually one ahead after Ps. 9 and vice versa. In MT, LXX, and Vulgate, the title of the Psalm is vv. 1.2, while the modern English versions, except *NAB,* omit the title from v. 1. As a result, vv. 2/3 in Hebrew is usually v. 1 in English (cf. 51:3 = 51:1).

3. The Formation of the Psalter

a. The Compilation of the Psalter

The Book of Psalms contains the compositions of many poets and singers whose works have been brought into a single volume. It contains centuries of devotion crammed into one book. In this respect, the Psalter is a microcosm of the Bible as a whole. One can trace four stages between composition and compilation of the psalms into a book: a) a psalm is composed; b) it is linked together with other psalms to form a small collection; c) several small collections are brought together to form a larger unit; d) the current Book of Psalms emerged, being a "collection of collections," with various individual psalms added by the editor(s) of the final book.[28]

A superficial observation of the Psalter reveals that it is artificially divided (89:52) into five books of varying lengths, each one ending with a doxology (41:13; 72:18-19; 89:52; 106:48):

> Book I: Psalms 1-41
> Book II: Psalms 42-72
> Book III: Psalms 73-89
> Book IV: Psalms 90-106
> Book V: Psalms 107-150[29]

This arrangement could possibly correspond to the five books of Moses, which were divided into 150 passages to be read in a three-year cycle. In that case, the 150 psalms would serve as responses to the above readings.

---

[28] Craigie, *Psalms,* 28.
[29] Leslie C. Allen, *Word Biblical Themes: Psalms* (Waco, TX: Word Books, 1987), 12-13; Craigie, *Psalms,* 30; J. David Pleins, *The Psalms* (Maryknoll, NY: Orbis Books, 1993).

b. Earlier Collections

Psalms existed far back in the history of Israel. The Israelites celebrated their victory at the Red Sea with hymns, the songs of Moses and Miriam (Ex. 15:1-18, 21), and the victory of Deborah and Barak over Jabin, the king of Canaan (Judg. 5:2-31). Even the prophetic books have their share of songs: Isa. 5:1-7, 23:16, 26:1-6, 27:2-5; Ezra 19:1-14; Hos. 6:1-3; Hab. 3. This process went on right up to the time of Christ. Many old psalms were lost, and some new psalms were composed even after the formation of the canon.

How the five books of the psalms were put together is a mystery. The Psalter in its present form is not the result of one single act of collection; nor has it been compiled throughout by the same people. Its present form represents the ultimate outcome of a process of collecting psalms. That it is a composite literary product is seen from the presence of duplicate Psalms (14 = 53; 70 = 40:13-17; 108 = 57:7-11 and 60:5-12) and from the existence of smaller collections or subordinate groupings within the book.

The first collection that strikes the eye is the Elohistic group (often called "Elohistic Psalter"), Ps. 42-83, where the name *YHWH* (Lord) is replaced by *Elohim* (God). The following is the distribution of the divine name in the Psalter:

Book I: 1-41: Yahweh 272 times, Elohim 15 times
II: 42-72: Yahweh 30 times, Elohim 164 times
III: 73-89: Yahweh 44 times, Elohim 43 times
IV: 90-106: Yahweh 103 times, Elohim never
V: 107-150: Yahweh 236 times, Elohim 7 times [30]

---

[30] Yahwist = southern (Judah) tradition (Jerusalem), Elohist = northern (Israel) tradition. The Elohistic revision is partial because the Psalter was perhaps not yet complete. For the signs of this

In the so-called "Elohistic Psalter," there are three smaller collections: that of Korah (Ps. 42-49)—the Korahites constituted a guild of temple singers (2 Chr. 20, 19); that of Asaph (Ps. 73-83), a cantor at the time of David (1 Chr. 25, 1-2); and that of David (Ps. 51-72).

In Ps. 3-41, 51-70, and 138-145, we find groupings of psalms "of David." Ps. 120-134 form the "Book of Pilgrim Songs" or "Songs of Ascents." Lastly, there is the collection of Hallel psalms: the *Egyptian Hallel Collection* (Ps. 113-118) and *Hallel Psalms* (146-150).[31]

The editor(s) of the Book of Psalms brought together the various collections and added a number of psalms, which were probably not included initially in a collection, to form the Psalter. Ps. 1 (perhaps also Ps. 2) was placed at the beginning as an introduction to the Psalter, and Ps. 50 formed a suitable conclusion.[32]

4. The Date

a. The Individual Psalms

The psalms we possess today were composed over a period of about 600 to 700 years. The prevailing opinion for some time was that of assigning a very late date to the majority of the psalms, even a Maccabean dating (after 105 BC). But the

---

editing: cf. 67:7, 43:4, 45:7, 50:7. The presence of the name *YHWH* in the psalms would point to their antiquity.

[31] Hallelujah = *hallelu+ jah* = praise Yah(weh) (= praise the Lord).

[32] Craigie, *Psalms*, 28-30. For another way of looking at the formation of the Psalter, cf. C. Westermann, *Praise and Lament in the Psalms* (Atlanta, 1981).

stylistic difference between the canonical psalms and the hymns discovered in Qumran leaves no doubt that there are no Maccabean songs in our Psalter. According to Dahood, the Ras Shamra texts show that much of the phraseology in the Psalter was current in Palestine long before the writing prophets. Also, the translators in the LXX betray an ignorance of biblical poetic idioms and biblical images and metaphors. It indicates a long chronological gap between the original composition of the psalms and their translation into Greek. Such considerations point to a pre-exilic date for most of the psalms (587 BC).[33]

b. The Final Collection

No precise information as to when the collection was completed is available. The process of collecting the psalms could possibly have begun in the Davidic period (c. 1012-972 BC). 2 Chr. 29:30 mentions the request of King Hezekiah (c. 715-685 BC) to the Levites to sing praises with the words of David and Asaph. After the exile, Nehemiah (c. 445-433 BC) founded a library and also collected the writing of David (2 Macc. 2:13). This process reached its culmination in the third century BC (c. 200 BC).[34] They were enshrined in the canon once and for all in c. AD 100.

---

[33]   Mitchell Dahood, *Psalms I: 1-50. A New Translation with Introduction and Commentary*, The Anchor Bible, 16 (New York: Doubleday, 1965), xxix-xxx; *Psalms III*, xxxiv-xxxvii; Artur Weiser, *The Psalms*, Old Testament Library (London: SCM Press, 1962), 91.

[34]   Cf. *The Prologue of Sirach*; completion of the LXX version.

5. Titles of the Psalms

a. Authorship

The thirty-four psalms in the MT (nineteen in LXX) without authors are called "orphans." But the majority of the psalms have titles. We do not, however, know much about the authors mentioned in them. Seventy-three psalms are attributed to David, twelve to Asaph, eleven to the sons of Korah, two to Solomon (Ps. 72, 127), and one each to Moses (Ps. 90), Heman (Ps. 88), and Ethan (Ps. 89) (cf. 1 Kgs 4:31; 1 Chr. 15:17-19, 25:5).

Traditionally, the phrase "a psalm of David" (*le dawid*) was considered to denote Davidic authorship. Certainly he possessed musical talent (1 Sam. 16:16-19), poetic gifts (2 Sam. 1:17-27, 3:33-34, 23:1-7), and a great love of liturgy (2 Sam. 6:5, 14-15; Ezra 3, 10; Neh. 12:24; Sir 47:8-10). Hence it is reasonable to think a few of his compositions formed the nucleus of the psalms attributed to him. But we have today no means of discovering exactly which they are.

Nevertheless, David could not have been the author of all the psalms attributed to him, because i) some of them contain references to the temple on Mt. Sion (24:7.9), and ii) the social and religious state of affairs presupposed in some others (exile, reconstruction of the walls of Jerusalem) point to a post-Davidic era (51:16-19). The ascription of psalms to David is to be understood, not in the proper sense of authorship, but in the style of the authorship of the Pentateuch by Moses or of the Wisdom Literature by Solomon (cf. the authorship of the *Dialogues* of Plato and the Book of Wisdom). "Hence," as Weiser states, "we must assume that the original purpose of the superscriptions of that kind was not at all to name the author of the psalm."[35] *Le dawid* would then more likely mean "belonging to the Davidic collection."

---

[35]   Weiser, *The Psalms,* 95.

The same is valid for the psalms attributed to Asaph and the sons of Korah. They probably originated in these guilds or were collected by them or were appointed to be sung by them.

b. Other Superscriptions

The following are some other superscriptions:

Indications regarding the musical instrument: "for the flutes" (Ps. 5)

The melody according to which the psalm is to be sung: "according to the Deer of the Dawn" (Ps. 22)

Terms indicating the category of the psalm: "a prayer" (Ps. 17), "a love song" (Ps. 45)

References to a historical situation: flight from Absolom (Ps. 3)

References to the occasion for which a psalm was composed: "A song at the dedication of the temple" (Ps. 30)

selah (Ps. 3): probably denotes a pause in music

miktam, penitential psalm or secret prayer: implies atonement (Ps. 16) or reconciliation (Ps. 56-60)

maskil, a didactic poem, instructive or artistic (Ps. 32)

alamoth (Ps. 46), *sheminith* (Ps. 6; 12 etc): probably signify the key to which the psalm in question was to be sung *te'pilla*, a lament or a plea

sir hamma'aloth (Songs of Ascents), songs of the returning exiles[36]

6. Hebrew Poetry

One-third of the OT text is poetic in form. Psalms, Proverbs, Song of Songs, Lamentations, Obadiah, Micah, Nahum, Habakkuk, and Zephaniah are fully poetry. Only seven books of the OT contain no poetry at all: Leviticus, Ruth, Ezra, Nehemiah, Esther, Haggai, and Malachi.

a. Parallelism

Parallelism is the most characteristic phenomenon of Hebrew poetry. Robert Lowth published his insights about this in 1753 in *Lectures on the Sacred Poetry of the Hebrews*. Lowth called the counterbalancing of verses *parallismus membrorum* (parallelism of members).

Parallelism consists in balancing thought against thought, phrase against phrase, word against word. In other words, it is saying the same thing twice in different words: "John was an old man, and an old man was he."

---

[36] For further information in this regard, cf. A. A. Anderson, *Psalms*, Vol. 1, *Psalms 1-72* (London: Oliphants, 1972); I. Engnell, *Critical Essays on the Old Testament*, 77-94; L. E. Keck, ed., *The Interpreter's Bible (NIB)*, Vol. 4 (Nashville, TN: Abingdon Press, 1996), 8-10; Yolanda Iglesias and Salvatore Putzu, *The Promise. An Introduction to the Old Testament* (Makati City, Philippines: Word and Life Publications, 1996), 150.

A principle of art is "the same in the other." This is present in the art of dance, architecture, and music. A parallelism has often been called a "thought rhyme," in which the poet is forced to give expression to the subject matter from different points of view (a blind man going to see the elephant). It offers the poet innumerable possibilities of inflection of poetic thought. His aim is not precision in the concepts but precision in the reproduction of the subject matter, if possible, over its whole range, precision not in the coining of terms but in the reproducing of facts:

"Have mercy on me, O God, according to your steadfast love; according to your abundant mercy blot out my transgressions" (Ps. 51:1).

For further examples, cf. Ps. 22:18, 37:6, 72:1, 109:14. "It is either a wonderful piece of luck or a wise provision of God's, that poetry which was turned into all languages should have as its chief formal characteristic one that does not disappear (as mere meter does) in translation."[37]

The basic unit of this type of poetic composition is a line or member (half or one-third of the parallelism), called technically a *stich* (*stichos* = row, line). When a verse consists of two lines or members, it is a *distich* (couplet: Ps. 51:1); if three, a *tristich* (triplet: Ps. 93:3).

There are three types of parallelism: a) synonymous (repetitive), b) antithetic (contrasting), and c) synthetic (progressive) (complementary) parallelisms.

---

37   C. S. Lewis, *Reflections on the Psalms* (Collins Fount Paperbacks, 1961), 12.

i. Synonymous (Repetitive) Parallelism

In a synonymous parallelism, the second and third member states approximately the same thing as the first member. In other words, the same thought or idea is repeated without significant addition or subtraction. It sustains and prolongs the effect of the first statement by recasting the notion in other words. The second line simply reinforces the first, so that its content is enriched, and the total effect becomes spacious and impressive.

The heavens are telling the glory of God and the firmament proclaims his handiwork (Ps. 19:1).

Other examples: Ps. 2:9, 24:1-3, 27:1, 37:1-30, 38:1, 49:1, 55:5, 103:10, 105:23, 132:2-5, 144:5; Prov. 16:1, 18:5, 19:5-15, 22:7.

Sometimes a synonymous parallelism is incomplete:

"The earth is the Lord's and all that is in it, the world,
and those who live in it" (24:1) (cf. Ps. 21:10, 6:2).

This type of parallelism is mainly due to a preference for variation, a delight in the manifold possibilities of inverted word order, of contraction or expansion of parallel terms.[38]

ii. Antithetic (Contrasting) Parallelism

Contrasting parallelism presents a contrast between the two members. It balances the stichs through opposition or contrast of thought (Ps. 20:7-8):

Some take pride in chariots and some in horses

---

[38] Chiastic parallelism: Ps. 22:18, Isa. 11:13b.

> But our pride is in the name of the Lord, our God.
> They will collapse and fall
> But we shall rise and stand upright.

For further examples, cf. Ps. 1:6, 27:10, 30:5, 32:10, 37:21, 90:6, 145:20; Prov. 10:5, 12:4, 13:12, 14:30; Magnificat (Lk. 1:52, 53).

There is an endless possibility of variation in this literary form. In each case, we have simply one possible contrary expression among many.

iii. Synthetic (Progressive/Formal/Numerical/Complimentary) Parallelism

Synthetic parallelism builds upon an earlier idea; that is, the second or third stich advances the thought of the first or second:

> O sing to the Lord a new song;
> Sing to the Lord, all the earth (Ps. 96:1).
> They have mouths, but they do not speak;
> they have eyes, but they do not see (Ps. 135:16).

For other examples, cf. Ps. 2:2, 6; 3:4; 14:1; 103:2; 103:3-5; 118:9; 127:1; Prov. 16:31, 17:2, 18:21; *Gloria in Excelsis* (Lk. 2:14).

There are many varieties of parallelism:

- In a relationship of question and answer: Ps. 119:9
- In a relationship of comparison: Ps. 118:8
- In a relationship of contrast: Ps. 118:18
- Three lines: synonymous (Ps. 93:3)
- First two lines: synonymous, and third line: synthetic (Ps. 2:2)
- First two lines: synonymous, and third line: antithetic (Ps. 54:3)

b. Meter

Meter is the arrangement of accented words that a given poem displays. The common pattern is the six-stress distich, represented as 3 + 3 meter:

> O give thanks/to the Lord/call on his name/
> make known/his deeds/among the peoples (Ps. 105:1)
> (cf. 95:2).

The other common meter, 3 + 2, is called the *quina,* or the lament meter:

> Hear a just/cause/O Lord
> Attend/to my cry (Ps. 17:1) (cf. Ps. 130:1).

There is also 2 + 2 meter:

> The Lord is/my shepherd,
> I shall not/want (Ps. 23:1).

c. Poetic Devices

Alliteration is a repetition of the same sound: "sing a song of sixpence," *shalu shelom yerushalaim* (Ps. 122:6a); *shiru lanu mishir Zion* (Ps. 137:3c).

An acrostic poem repeats the same letter at the beginning of a verse or stanza in the order of the letters of the alphabet: Ps. 9-10, 25, 34, 37, 111, 112, 119,[39] 145.

---

[39] Ps. 119 consists of twenty-two strophes of eight lines each of the twenty-two Hebrew alphabets.

Inclusion means that the author returns to the point he started with: Ps. 8:1-9.

Other devices include simile (Ps. 22:12-16, 102:6-7), metaphor (Ps. 144:5-7, 22:12-13, 3:3), personification (Ps. 19:1-2),[40] picturesque language (Ps. 3:7), and hyperbole (Ps. 3:6).[41]

7. The Psalter and the Rest of the OT

Martin Luther called the Psalter "a Bible in miniature." To Robert Bellarmine, it was *"quasi compendium et summa totius Veteris Testamenti"* ("a compendium and summary of the whole OT"). In fact, the Psalter can be called a microcosm of the OT.

The Book of Psalms sums up in its own poetical fashion the doctrine, history, and revelation contained in the Torah, the Prophets, and the Writings. A fairly good background knowledge of these sections of the Bible (there is no such thing as Psalms without tears!) is a *sine qua non* for understanding and appreciating the condensed statements, the allusions, the poetic imagery of these songs. As French scholar Andre Robert put it, "The Book of Psalms enables us to hear an echo of the entire Bible, whose doctrine it expresses in prayer."

The Hebrews possessed a unique sense of history. Their history was written by a God who revealed himself to them through his interventions in their favour. So close was his relationship to them that he was called a father (Ex. 4:22, Hos. 11:1), a husband (Hos. 2:16), a king, a shepherd, and a judge. The central events

---

[40]   See J. Clinton McCann Jr., "Psalms for Moderns: Picture Prayer," *Sursum Corda* 11 (1970-1971): 15-22.

[41]   Jerome F. D. Creach, *Interpretation Bible Studies: Psalms* (Louisville, KY: Westminster John Knox Press, 1998), 9.

in their history were the exodus, the gift of the land, and the institution of the monarchy. The main themes contained in the Psalms—deliverance, covenant, law (God's greatest gift to Israel, a gift by which his will was revealed to them), land, kingship, temple, and holy city—revolve around the three great events mentioned above. What is most consoling is that these acts of Yahweh became for them (consequently, for us as well) patterns or paradigms of his future interventions in history.

8. Psalms and the Cult

One of the disputed issues that arose as a by-product of the form-critical study of the Psalms is that of their *Sitz im Leben* (life setting). In particular, what is the relationship of the psalms to the cult in Israel? What forms did this take in her history?

It is generally admitted that in the study of the psalms, one has to keep constantly in mind the history of the OT cultus. Some would go to the extent of affirming that "the cultus was the native soil from which the psalms sprung."[42]

According to Sigmund Mowinckel (1884-1966), "cult or ritual may be defined as the socially established and regulated holy acts and words in which the encounter and communion of the deity with the congregation is established, developed, and brought to its ultimate goal. In other words: a relation in which a religion becomes a vitalising function as a communion of God and congregation, and of the members of the congregation amongst themselves."[43] In the cult, the acts and words express what takes place. The words produce the blessings pronounced, just as a curse brings malediction.

---

[42]   Weiser, *The Psalms*, 24.

[43]   Sigmund Mowinckel, *The Psalms in Israel's Worship*, trans. D. R. Ap-Thomas (Nashville, TN: Abingdon, 1962), 15.

Hermann Gunkel (1862-1932) wrote that many of the psalms were used in worship services in the Jerusalem cult. Each type of psalm originally had a specific function, and it had to do with certain ceremonies of the national festivals and celebrations.

His position was considered unsatisfactory by later scholars who, in their turn, concentrated on a particular cultic festival as the seed-bed on which sprung many psalms:

(i) To Mowinckel, a number of psalms (about forty) were composed for and used in the annual ritual enthronement of Yahweh as king during the autumn festival. He called it the feast of the Enthronement of YHWH. The main elements of this cultic drama are the following: i) a sacred procession around the temple carrying the Ark (throne of YHWH); ii) the dramatisation of the triumph of Yahweh over the mythological and historical enemies of creation and Israel; and iii) the proclamation and celebration of Yahweh's assumption and reign as king over creation, the world, and Israel.

(ii) Artur Weiser, in contrast with Mowinckel, explains the psalms in the light of a reconstructed Israeli covenant festival. The dominant theology in ancient Israel was covenantal. "Hence the cult of this festival must be assumed to be the *Sitz im Leben* for the vast majority of the individual psalms and their types."[44]

(iii) A third alternative is offered by Hans-Joachim Kraus. He points to a royal Zion festival, which focuses upon the establishment of the Yahwistic cult in Jerusalem and the founding of the Davidic dynasty.

---

[44] Weiser, *The Psalms*, 35. For further information, cf. ibid., 35-52.

Evaluating the various theories referred to up to now, the following facts deserve to be kept in mind:

i) The psalms, in their original usage, should be understood against the actual realities of cultic worship.

ii) They were, however, made use of in the context of diverse and complex cultic activities. As a result, it is difficult for us to reconstruct—though some of their vestiges are available to us from different sources—much of the supposed cultic context involved.

iii) The present day psalms have lost their association with their original *Sitz im Leben*. They had their own history of interpretations and reinterpretations before they came to our possession.

In sum, the psalms reflect, are designed for, and belong to the recurring situations in the life of the community. They picture the ongoing life and faith of Israel.

9. The Theology of the Psalms

The Psalter "might well be called a little Bible . . . . Anyone who could not read the whole Bible would here have anyway almost an entire summary of it, comprised in one single book" (Martin Luther). In a similar way the theology of the psalms could be called "a biblical theology in miniature."[45] The psalms fall into that category of literature in the OT that seems to be primarily of human creation. The Book of Psalms contains Israel's songs and prayers, which constitute the response of the chosen people to the revelation they have received from God. This provides a starting point for all theological reflection on the Book of Psalms.

---

[45]   Kraus, *Theology of the Psalms,* 12.

The theological richness of the psalms emerges out of the deep personal relationship between God and Israel. The framework for all dimensions of that relationship is provided by the covenant. The psalmists can be called covenant writers. Their knowledge of God is rooted in the covenant. They respond to God in prayer, in praise, or in particular life situations. Because of this way of functioning, we can state that all the psalms are covenant oriented. As the covenant dominated all aspects of life, there will not be any aspect of life that does not appear in the psalms. They are related to coronation (Ps. 2), personal prayer (Ps. 3), praise of God in a storm (Ps. 29), wonders of creation (Ps. 104), particular religious festivals (Ps. 113-118), and so on. This shows that the psalms contain popular theology. Such theology or knowledge of God emerges out of a life lived in relationship with God. Popular theology is theology at its best, for if knowledge of God is revealed to all humankind, then that knowledge should be grasped and articulated by all. The Book of Psalms offers this theology for all to utilise. This theology has survived.[46]

In the interpretation of the psalms, we can try to distinguish between different layers of theological meaning and significance. Ps. 2 was initially a royal psalm related to the coronation of a Davidic king. Later, when there were no kings, the function of the psalm was broadened to a more general function in the context of Israel's worship. By NT times, Ps. 2 was clearly recognised as messianic, thereby gaining a new dimension in its meaning: "The words of the psalm do not change, but its function and significance have changed over the passage of time. Consequently there is a change, or at least development, in the theological significance of the psalm; whereas in its original form, its theology pertained to the role of God in relation to the Davidic kings, that theology eventually blossomed into a fully

---

[46] [46] Craigie, *Psalms*, 39-40.

messianic theology in one period of the history of the psalm's interpretation. The latter stage is not a new theology, but a growth and development from the initial nucleus."[47]

When we look at the psalm from this point of view, two aspects are to be kept in mind: 1) To understand a psalm fully, begin by determining its initial meaning, the initial theological significance of the psalm. 2) The reinterpretation of the individual psalms within the biblical tradition can lead us to contemporary reinterpretation of the psalm for our own use. There are theological problems if we attempt to make the psalms relevant and meaningful for today. There are difficulties with regard to some individual laments. They are not to be taken as oracles of God. They are reactions to painful realities of human life. Yet they open a window to the soul of the psalmist. These reactionary sentiments are the real and natural reactions to the experience of evil and pain. These sentiments are part of the life of the soul that is bared before God in worship and prayer. The psalmist may hate his oppressor; God hates the oppression. A psalm may reflect the intimacy of the relationship between the psalmist and God. The expression of hatred is in a way a confession of sin, a part of the inner life of a person that may be cleansed and transformed through the relationship with God.[48]

The theological heart of the Psalter is that the Lord reigns (Ps. 93-99). On it depends our "happiness," "righteousness," life, and future. This affirmation—the Lord reigns—pervades the Psalter. God is frequently addressed as "King" (Ps. 5:2; 10:16; 24:7-10; 29:10; 44:4; 47:2, 7; 48:2; 68:24; 74:12; 84:3; 95:3; 98:6; 145:1; 149:2). These royal psalms serve to articulate God's sovereignty. The songs of Zion are also affirmations of God's universal reign. Jerusalem has become a concrete symbol of the extension of

---

47   Craigie, *Psalms,* 40-41.
48   Craigie, *Psalms,* 41.

God's rule in all places and times. This affirms God's cosmic reign. The Psalter even proclaims God's universal reign amid circumstances that seem to deny it. Happiness (Ps. 1:1, 2:12), prosperity (Ps. 1:3), and refuge (Ps. 2:12) exist not beyond but rather in the midst of opposition and suffering. The dominant voice in the Psalter is that of prayer. It is a way of life for those who entrust themselves fully to God's care.[49]

Prayer and praise are inseparable in the Psalter. While prayer is the offering of the whole self to God through direct address, involving even complaint, confession of sin or innocence, and so on, praise is the offering of the whole self to God through affirmation of his sovereignty and enthusiastic celebration of God's character and activity. This attitude implies that the whole cosmos and all its peoples, creatures, and things belong to God. Ecology and theology are inseparable. To live under God's rule is to live in partnership with all other species and in partnership with the church itself (Ps. 8, 19, 29, 104, 147, 148).[50]

The most important theological concept in the Book of Psalms is "steadfast love" or "unfailing love" (*hesed*). The chosen people appeal to God's steadfast love in prayer (Ps. 6, 13, 31, 44, 51, 63), and Israel celebrates God's unfailing love in songs of praise (Ps. 33, 100, 103, 136, 145, 147). God shows himself to be "merciful and gracious, slow to anger, and abounding in steadfast love and faithfulness" (Ex. 34:6). Psalms convey God's motherly compassion (Ps. 25:6, 40:11, 51:1, 69:16, 78:8, 106:45, 111:4). God's "steadfast love" appears and virtually serves as a summary of Israel's understanding of the character of God.[51]

---

[49]   J. Clinton McCann Jr., "The Book of Psalms," in *NIB*, Vol., 666-669.

[50]   Ibid., 669-670.

[51]   Ibid., 670-671.

The Psalter recognises the wrath of God (Ps. 2:5, 12). Among the psalms there are appeals to God's wrath against their enemies (Ps. 56:7, 59:13), and the Israelites are aware of experiencing God's wrath (Ps. 6:1; 38:1; 78:59, 62; 88:7, 16; 89:38, 46; 90:7, 9, 11). But how can God be loving and wrathful, gracious and just, forgiving and punishing? It is a question that cannot easily be answered. This dilemma is the result of God being able to love a sinful race, and it reveals God's willingness to be vulnerable and to suffer for love's sake. God's justice is ultimately manifest as love. The mystery of the sovereignty of God made perfect in steadfast love comes into sharpest focus on the cross of Jesus Christ.[52]

10. The Psalms and the New Testament

The early church used the psalms both as liturgical materials and as a theological resource. Evidence of the liturgical use is found in Paul's advice to the Colossians to "sing psalms, hymns, and spiritual songs to God" (Col. 3:16, Eph. 5:19). New psalms were written and sung in the early Christian communities. These "spiritual songs" may refer to Christian materials created with inspiration from the psalms, for example, the *Magnificat* (Lk. 1:46-55), which contains echoes of Ps. 98 and 113, and the Song of Simeon (Lk. 2:28-32), which echoes Ps. 119:123. The Psalter is the ground from which the language of the Spirit-inspired hymns and prayer songs of early Christianity sprung.

The early Christians also used the psalms as a theological resource. The psalms are quoted or alluded to in the NT more than any other OT book. The theology of the psalms is in agreement with the core of Jesus' teaching and preaching. The theological heart of the Psalter—God reigns—is precisely

---

[52]   Ibid., 671-672.

the fundamental good news that Jesus announces (see Mk 1:14-15). Jesus proclaimed the reign of God as a present reality, and people were invited to enter it and experience it. God's reign, his sovereignty, is not the demonstration of sheer power but the embodiment of sheer love. The involvement of God with humanity is completed in Jesus' ministry of suffering servant-hood. The early Christians saw in Jesus the culmination of the monarchical ideal of the psalms. The cross was the clearest demonstration of God's character and sovereignty; Jesus shared his ministry of suffering servant-hood with his followers (Mk 8:34). The followers' lives, like Jesus' own life, will replicate the lives of the psalmists who are "happy" in the midst of their constant affliction.

The Gospel writers frequently refer or allude to the psalms when they tell the story of Jesus. Luke's account of Jesus' birth (Lk. 2:13-14) recalls the content and movement of Ps. 29. The heavenly voice at Jesus' baptism (Mt. 3:17, Mk 1:11, Lk. 3:22) quotes a portion of Ps. 2:7. This text is cited again at Jesus' transfiguration (Mt. 17:5, Mk 9:7, Lk. 9:35). In the narrative of the passion of Jesus, the Gospel writers rely most heavily on the psalms. Jesus' entry into Jerusalem (Mt. 21:9, Mk 11:9-10, Lk. 19:38, Jn 12:12) is narrated with reference to Ps. 118. Ps. 22 shapes the account of the crucifixion in all four Gospels, and in Mt. 27:46 and Mk 15:34, the words of Jesus from the cross are a quotation of Ps. 22:1. Jesus' final words in Luke (Lk. 23:46) are from Ps. 35:5, and in John (Jn 19:30), they allude perhaps to Ps. 31:5 and 22:31. These are lament psalms. The passion accounts have been influenced by Ps. 69. So Jesus is presented as the ultimate paradigm of the faithful sufferer. The cross is, for the Christians, the ultimate revelation of the mystery the psalms present, that is, divine sovereignty manifested in perfect love.[53]

---

53   Ibid., 672-674.

As the lament and praise are inseparable in the psalms, so is the relation between the cross and the resurrection to be seen in the NT. The first recorded Christian sermon, Peter's sermon on the Day of Pentecost (Acts 2:25-36), is based primarily on Ps. 16:8-11, 110:1, and 132:11. Ps. 110 is often quoted or alluded to in articulating the glory of the crucified one (see 1 Cor. 15:25; Eph. 1:20; Col. 3:1; Heb. 1:3, 8:1, 10:12-13, 12:2).

In the NT, God's justice is ultimately manifested as grace. It implies affirmation of life for all people, not based on any system of human merit but as a result of God's loving gift. The message is again congruent with that of the psalms, and Paul appeals to the psalms to support his case. In Rom. 3:9-20, Paul cites several psalms, including Ps. 14:1-3 and 143:2. This theology of divine justice revealed as gracious love, found in the psalms and in Jesus, led Paul to open the church to all people (see Rom. 15:9-11, which quotes Ps. 89:49 and 117:1).

The Book of Revelation (2:26-27) quotes directly Ps. 2:8-9. Direct quotations like this are rare in this book, but it is full of singing and songs that could well have been inspired by the Psalter. The Revelation shares the Psalter's fundamental conviction that God rules the world, and the mention of "a new song" (Rev. 5:9, 14:3) explicitly recalls Ps. 96, 98, and 149.[54] Psalms are found in Rev. 5:9-10, 11:17-18, 12:10-12, 19:6-8).

There are many quotations of psalms in the NT. The clearest identification is in Acts 13:33 of Ps. 2:7. In Lk. 20:42-43 and Acts 1:20, there are clear references to the psalms. Quotations in the NT of Ps. 2, 22, 69, 110, and 118 were of particular importance for the kerygma of the early church. Ps. 2 and 110 are royal psalms.

---

54 Ibid., 674-675.

Ps. 2 is quoted in the NT in connection with the baptism of Jesus and his transfiguration (Mt. 3:17, 17:5; Mk 9:7; Lk. 3:22, 9:35; 2 Pet. 1:17). Ps. is also quoted in Acts (4:25-26, 13:33), in the letter to the Hebrews (1:5, 5:5, 7:28), and in Revelation (2:26-27; 6:15; 11:15, 18; 17:18; 19:19). Two themes are stressed in these references: divine sonship (based on Ps. 2:7) and the rebellion and defeat of the hostile nations (Ps. 2:1-2, 8-9). "You are my son, today I have begotten you" (Ps. 2:7). The ruler of Israel was installed by Yahweh as his "son," as the representative of divine power and majesty. Thus the adoption took on the meaning of a choosing of the king. The chosen *messiah* (anointed) (Ps. 2:2) is placed at Yahweh's side as one nearest to him, as the "heir" of the realm of divine glory (Ps. 2:8-9). There was a deep relationship between God and the king. This idea of the king was transferred to the *messiah*.

Ps. 2:7 is quoted in the NT texts that deal with the exultation of the messiah into God's heavenly world (Heb. 1:5, 5:5, 7:28). Heb. 1:8-9 adds to the citation of Ps. 2:7 a passage from Ps. 45:7-8, a royal psalm. This expresses clearly that Christ, as the exalted Son of God, is God. Thus "God" in Ps. 45:7 is understood as a reference to the deity of the ruler. This context emphasises that as "Son of God," he is truly God, and his kingdom is the kingdom of God. Heb. 5:5 combines Ps. 2:7 and Ps. 110:4. Christ is installed as high priest by the conferral of power in Ps. 2:7, and so he has been appointed as priest forever after the order of Melchizedek (Heb. 5:6). In Heb. 7:28, the two psalms are brought together into the form "Son . . . for ever."

Ps. 110 played an extraordinary role in the early church. Ps. 110:1 and 4 are cited in the letter to the Hebrews. The emphasis in it is to the fact that Christ has been made a high priest after the order of Melchizedek (Heb. 5:6, 10; 6:20; 7:3; 11:15, 17, 21, 24, 28). The sovereign authority of the exalted one is proven by the quotation of Ps. 110:4. Heb. 7:3 takes up the older Melchizedek tradition from Gen. 14:20. What Ps. 110 says about the priest-king is used in Hebrews to bear testimony to the honour of the heavenly high priest, who has been taken up into the world of God. Both Ps. 110:1 and 4 play an important role in the letter to the Hebrews. Christ as the "heir" (Ps. 2:8) has sat down "at the right hand of God" on high (Heb. 1:3). When we combine Ps. 110:1 and Ps. 110:4, we have a concept of a high priest who sits at the right hand of God in heaven (Heb. 8:11).

From the category of prayer songs of the individual, which address Yahweh in the midst of great peril, the NT refers especially to Ps. 22 and 69. "My God, my God, why hast thou forsaken me?" (Ps. 22:1) are the last words of Jesus spoken on the cross (Mk 15:34, Mt. 27:46), only the statement from the psalm is cited in Hebrew. The psalms of the OT were the prayer book of Jesus. The cry contained in Ps. 22:1 is a cry that belongs to the unforgettable remembrances of what occurred. It gives voice to the terrifying lament of one who has been forsaken by God. In the passion narrative of the NT, the prayer song Ps. 69 plays a significant role. Ps. 69:21, "They gave me poison for food, and for my thirst they gave me vinegar to drink," is quoted in Mk 15:36; Mt. 27:34, 48; Lk. 23:36; and Jn 19:29.

Ps. 118, cited in the NT, had a great significance in Judaism. The petition "hosanna," "save us" (Ps. 118:25), was a cultic formula used in the Feast of Tabernacles. Ps. 113-118, known as the Egyptian Hallel, were a fixed part of the Jewish cycle of autumn feasts and of Passover. In Judaism, Ps. 118:22-23 was interpreted as referring to Abraham, David, and the Messiah. A Messianic interpretation of the psalm was in the air. Ps. 118:22-23: "The stone which the builders rejected has become the cornerstone" (Mt. 21:42, Lk. 20:17). The Messiah who was rejected and killed by his own people carries and supports the people of God. Ps. 118:25-26 is connected with Mt. 23:39, 13:35, 19:38, 21:9, 15; Mk 11:9-10; and Jn 12:13. "Hosanna" is taken up in the pericope of Jesus' entry into Jerusalem.

There are unmistakable allusions to the Psalter in the NT. The psalms are found most frequently in the Book of Revelation, in the letters of Paul, in the Synoptic Gospels, and in the Acts of the Apostles.[55]

---

[55]   Kraus, *Theology of the Psalms,* 177-181, 183-185, 188, 191, 193-194.

CLASSIFICATION AND EXPOSITION OF THE PSALMS

1. Approaches to Psalms Study

In the past, various methods have been employed in the study of the psalms:

Some studied them as religious and poetic compositions expressive of individual piety. An outstanding example of this approach is found in A. F. Kirkpatrick's *The Book of Psalms* (1902). To him the Psalter is a collection of religious lyrics that express the personal emotions of the poet. It is the thought of God that stirs up the emotions that, in their turn, are directed God-wards.

Others focused their attention on the historical concerns in the psalms. They tried to assign to each psalm its exact historical context and to analyse it for traces of historical connections. Two of the proponents of this approach are C. A. Briggs's *The Book of Psalms* (1906-1907) and Moses Buttenweiser's *The Psalms: Chronologically Treated with a New Translation* (1938). The latter even attempted to give a precise date to every psalm.

Hermann Gunkel's form-critical approach to the psalms[56] is the one that is most widely used today. He pioneered the method of study called *form-criticism*. He identified and described the basic types or genres (*Gattungen*) in the psalms. He also tried to identify the individual or communal life situations (*Sitz im Leben*) in which those types functioned. The psalm types proposed by Gunkel are the following: 1) hymns; 2) communal laments; 3) royal psalms; 4) individual laments; and 5) individual songs of thanksgiving, and a number of minor categories: i) pilgrimage songs; ii) wisdom poetry; iii) communal songs of thanksgiving; and iv) liturgy.

Gunkel's method has been subsequently touched up, extended, and refined by a host of scholars. Mowinckel,[57] an outstanding representative and another pioneer of psalm criticism, sought to establish the cultic background of the Psalter. He dealt with the relationship between the psalms and Israel's cult through a *cult-historical* method. He argued that a number of psalms must be related to an Israeli New Year festival.

Artur Weiser[58] found a focus for psalm interpretation in the covenant, specifically in his understanding of the "covenant festival." The covenant festival is perceived to have been the central and most comprehensive celebration in Israeli life, centered on Israel's annual reestablishment of its formal alliance with the Lord. Weiser proposes that the majority of the psalms find their life setting in the covenant festival.

---

[56]   H. Gunkel, *The Psalms: A Form-Critical Introduction*, trans. T. M. Horner (Philadelphia: Fortress, 1967), 10-39.

[57]   Mowinckel, *Psalms in Israel's Worship*.

[58]   Weiser, *The Psalms*.

H.-J. Kraus[59] refined the form-critical method and took account of the data provided by archaeological research since Gunkel's time. His work also exhibits a somewhat more explicit theological perspective than was evinced in the writings of Gunkel. Claus Westermann[60] emphasises the movement in the Psalter from lament, which dominates the first part of the Psalter, to praise, which dominates its latter part. The types of *form-critical* study were developed by Gunkel and refined by Kraus and Westermann.

Some recent approaches to the psalms contain newer emphases. Within the context of French biblical scholarship, there has appeared a form of analysis by which a *relecture* ("rereading") of a psalm is done. The original specific purpose of the psalm might be modified for different use in a later life situation.[61]

Dahood[62] has presented a new translation of the psalms that is very much dependent on Ugaritic. His work on the psalms is the most radical and far-reaching in its implications since the time of Gunkel.

The works of Gunkel and Mowinckel have been invaluable in many respects. Weiser's stress on the covenant has also been recognised as being of considerable importance. With Dahood, we have to recognise Ugaritic as being of great importance in the study of the psalms.[63]

---

[59]   Hans-Joachim Kraus, *Psalms 1-59 and Psalms 60-150. A Commentary,* trans. Hilton C. Oswald (Minneapolis: Augsburg Publishing House, 1988).

[60]   Westermann, *Praise and Lament in the Psalms.*

[61]   E. Beaucamp, *Le Psautier. Ps. 1-72.* SB 7 (Paris: Gabalda, 1976).

[62]   Mitchell Dahood, *Psalms I. 1-50. Introduction, Translations and Notes.* AB 16 (New York: Doubleday, 1966).

[63]   Craigie, *Word Biblical Commentary: Psalms 1-50,* 45-48.

2. Classification of the Psalms

Psalmody in Israel was undoubtedly influenced by Egyptian and Babylonian prototypes. The psalmists composed their songs on the model of acknowledged literary forms (types) (*Gattung*, genre). Each type had its own setting in life (*Sitz im Leben*), usually liturgical.

Based on the criteria of a certain recognisable uniformity of style, recurrent motifs, grammatical indications, and so on, the psalms can be divided into the following principal types: hymns (descriptive praise), thanksgiving psalms (declarative praise), lament psalms, and wisdom (didactic) psalms. The thanksgiving and lament could be either of an individual or of the nation. Points of contact are perceptible between these and other categories. The royal psalms, psalms of Yahweh's kingship, songs of Zion, and pilgrim psalms have some elements in common with the hymns. Songs of confidence (trust) are related to the lament.

According to Claus Westermann's *Praise and Lament in the Psalms*, the whole Psalter can be split into songs of praise and laments. He subdivided the songs of praise into descriptive praise (hymns) and declarative praise (thanksgiving).

The following is a detailed classification of the psalms. But it can never do full justice to the diversity found within the Psalter. Scholars are not unanimous as to the types as well as the individual psalms assigned to each type. In certain cases, the content also has been into consideration in the process that led to their classification:

PSALMS CLASSIFIED

Ps. 1: Wisdom Psalm

Ps. 2: Royal Psalm

Ps. 3: Individual Lament

Ps. 4: Individual Lament

Ps. 5: Individual Lament

Ps. 6: Individual Lament

Ps. 7: Individual Lament

Ps. 8: Hymn

Ps. 9 (9A): Individual
Thanksgiving Psalm

Ps. 10 (9B): Individual Lament

Ps. 11 (10): Psalm of Trust

Ps. 12 (11): Individual Lament

Ps. 13 (12): Individual Lament

Ps. 14 (13): Individual Lament

Ps. 15 (14): Pilgrim Psalm

Ps. 16 (15): Psalm of Trust

Ps. 17 (16): Individual Lament

Ps. 18 (17): Individual
Thanksgiving

Ps. 19 (18): A—Hymn;
B—Wisdom Psalm

Ps. 20 (19): Royal Psalm

Ps. 21 (20): Royal Psalm

Ps. 22 (21): Individual Lament

Ps. 23 (22): Psalm of Trust

Ps. 24 (23): Pilgrim Psalm

Ps. 25 (24): Individual Lament

Ps. 26 (25): Individual Lament

Ps. 27 (26): Individual Lament

Ps. 28 (27): Individual Lament

Ps. 29 (28): Hymn

Ps. 30 (29): Individual
Thanksgiving

Ps. 31 (30): Individual Lament

Ps. 32 (31): Individual
Thanksgiving

Ps. 33 (32): Hymn

Ps. 34 (33): Individual
Thanksgiving

Ps. 35 (34): Individual Lament

Ps. 36 (35): Individual Lament

Ps. 37 (36): Wisdom Psalm

Ps. 38 (37): Individual Lament

Ps. 39 (38): Individual Lament

Ps. 40 (39): Individual
Thanksgiving

Ps. 41 (40): Individual
Thanksgiving

Ps. 42 (41): Individual
Thanksgiving

Ps. 43 (42): Individual
Thanksgiving

Ps. 44 (43): National Lament

Ps. 45 (44): Royal Psalm

Ps. 46 (45): Song of Zion

Ps. 47 (46): Yahweh's Kingship

Ps. 48 (47): Song of Zion

Ps. 49 (48): Wisdom Psalm

Ps. 50 (49): Pilgrim Psalm

Ps. 51 (50): Individual Lament

Ps. 52 (51): Individual Lament

Ps. 53 (52): Individual Lament

Ps. 54 (53): Individual Lament

Ps. 55 (54): Individual Lament

Ps. 56 (55): Individual Lament

Ps. 57 (56): Individual Lament

Ps. 58 (57): Individual Lament

Ps. 59 (58): Individual Lament

Ps. 60 (59): National Lament

Ps. 61 (60): Individual Lament

Ps. 62 (61): Psalm of Trust

Ps. 63 (62): Psalm of Trust

Ps. 64 (63): Individual Lament

Ps. 65 (64): National
Thanksgiving

Ps. 66A (65A): National Thanksgiving;

66B (65B): Individual Thanksgiving

Ps. 67 (66): National Thanksgiving

Ps. 68 (67): Pilgrim Psalm

Ps. 69 (68): Individual Lament

Ps. 70 (69): Individual Lament

Ps. 71 (70): Individual Lament

Ps. 72 (71): Royal Psalm

Ps. 73 (72): Wisdom Psalm

Ps. 74 (73): National Lament

Ps. 75 (74): National Thanksgiving

Ps. 76 (75): Song of Zion

Ps. 77 (76): Individual Lament

Ps. 78 (77): Historical Psalm

Ps. 79 (78): National Lament

Ps. 80 (79): National Lament

Ps. 81 (80): Pilgrim Psalm

Ps. 82 (81): Oracles of Judgment

Ps. 83 (82): National Lament

Ps. 84 (83): Pilgrim Psalm

Ps. 85 (84): National Lament

Ps. 86 (85): Individual Lament

Ps. 87 (86): Song of Zion

Ps. 88 (87): Individual Lament

Ps. 89 (88): Individual Lament

Ps. 90 (89): National Lament

Ps. 91 (90): Psalm of Trust

Ps. 92 (91): Hymn

Ps. 93 (92): Yahweh's Kingship

Ps. 94 (93): Individual Lament

Ps. 95 (94): Yahweh's Kingship

Ps. 96 (95): Yahweh's Kingship

Ps. 97 (96): Yahweh's Kingship

Ps. 98 (97): Yahweh's Kingship

Ps. 99 (98): Yahweh's Kingship

Ps. 100 (99): Hymn

Ps. 101 (100): Royal Psalm

Ps. 102 (101): Individual
Lament

Ps. 103 (102): Individual
Thanksgiving

Ps. 104 (103): Hymn

Ps. 105 (104): Historical Psalm

Ps. 106 (105): Historical Psalm

Ps. 107 (106): National
Thanksgiving

Ps. 108 (107): National Lament

Ps. 109 (108): Individual
Lament

Ps. 110 (109): Royal Psalm

Ps. 111 (110): Hymn

Ps. 112 (111): Wisdom Psalm

Ps. 113 (112): Hymn

Ps. 114 (113A): Hymn

Ps. 115 (113B): National Lament

Ps. 116A (114): Individual
Thanksgiving

Ps. 116B (115): Individual
Thanksgiving

Ps. 117 (116): Hymn

Ps. 118 (117): Individual
Thanksgiving

Ps. 119 (118): Wisdom Psalm

Ps. 120 (119): Individual
Lament

Ps. 121 (120): Psalm of Trust

Ps. 122 (121): Pilgrim Psalm

Ps. 123 (122): National Lament

Ps. 124 (123): National
Thanksgiving

Ps. 125 (124): National Lament

Ps. 126 (125): National
Thanksgiving

Ps. 127 (126): Wisdom Psalm

Ps. 128 (127): Wisdom Psalm

Ps. 129 (128): National Lament

Ps. 130 (129): Individual
Lament

Ps. 131 (130): Psalm of Trust

Ps. 132 (131): Royal Psalm

Ps. 133 (132): Wisdom Psalm

Ps. 134 (133): Liturgical
Blessing

Ps. 135 (134): Hymn

Ps. 136 (135): Hymn

Ps. 137 (136): National Lament

Ps. 138 (137): National
Thanksgiving

Ps. 139 (138): Individual
Lament (Wisdom Psalm)

Ps. 140 (139): Individual
Lament

Ps. 141 (140): Individual
Lament

Ps. 142 (141): Individual
Lament

Ps. 143 (142): Individual
Lament

Ps. 144 (143): Individual
Lament

Ps. 145 (144): Hymn

Ps. 146 (145): Hymn

Ps. 147a (146): Hymn

Ps. 147B (147): Hymn

Ps. 148: Hymn

Ps. 149: Hymn

Ps. 150: Hymn

1. Hymns of Praise (descriptive praise): 8, 19a, 29, 33, 92, 100, 104, 111, 113, 114, 117, 135-136, 145-150
2. Psalms of Trust (confidence): 4, 11, 16, 23, 27, 62, 63, 91, 121, 131
3. Thanksgiving Psalms (declarative praise):

   a) Individual (personal, private): 9, 18, 30, 32, 34, 40, 41, 66b, 103, 116, 118, 138
   b) National (communal): 65, 66a, 67, 75, 107, 124, 126

4. Royal Psalms: 2, 20, 21, 45, 72, 101, 110, 132
5. Psalms of Yahweh's Kingship (enthronement psalms): 47, 93, 95, 96-99
6. Songs of Zion: 46, 48, 76, 87
7. Pilgrim Psalms: 15, 24, 50, 81, 84, 95, 122
8. Lament (petition; entreaty; suffering):

   a) Individual (personal): 3, 4, 5-7, 10, 12-14, 17, 22, 25-28, 31, 35, 36, 38, 39, 41, 42, 45, 51-59, 61, 64, 69, 71, 77, 86, 88, 89, 94, 102, 109, 120, 130, 139, 140-44
   b) National: 44, 60, 74, 79, 80, 83, 85, 90, 115, 123, 125, 129, 137

9. Wisdom Psalms (psalms about the righteous and the sinner): 1, 19b, 37, 49, 73, 112, 119, 127; 128, 133, 139
10. Historical Psalms: 78, 105, 106

I. DESCRIPTIVE PSALMS OF PRAISE (HYMNS)

1. What Is It?

The most exuberant, extensive, and expansive indicators of who and what God is, and what God is about, are also found and elaborated in the hymns. In the hymns of Israel, the most elemental structure of Old Testament faith is set forth. Praise is language of God and about God.[64] One can trace the existence of hymns to the earliest traditions of Israel, as in the cases of the canticle of Miriam (Ex. 15) and the song of Deborah (Judg. 5). A hymn (*tehillah*, from *hala*, "Sing a Song") is a song of praise that glorifies God as God. It celebrates the exclusive glory of Yahweh as revealed in nature and in history, especially in the history of Israel. The content of the hymn remains Yahweh's majesty and, as Gunkel writes, "in these songs we are confronted with the total power and majesty of the God of Israel."[65]

The hymns are pure praise. Petition generally finds no place in them. "The basic moods of these poems are enthusiasm, adoration, reverence, praise, and laudation."[66] The same line of thinking is found in Mowinckel: "The core of the hymn of praise is the consciousness of the poet and congregation that they are standing face to face with the Lord himself, meeting the almighty, holy, and merciful God in his own place, and worshiping him with praise and adoration."[67]

---

[64]   Patrick D. Miller, Jr., *Interpreting the Psalms* (Philadelphia: Fortress Press, 1986), 64.

[65]   Gunkel, *The Psalms*, 30.

[66]   H. Gunkel and J. Begrich, *Einleitung in die Psalmen*, 68.

[67]   Mowinckel, *The Psalms in Israel's Worship*, I, 81.

For Westermann in *Praise and Lament in the Psalms of the OT*,[68] psalms of praise take two forms: declarative (*toda*) and descriptive (*tehillah*) praise. Declarative praise (thanksgiving psalms) is the recounting in praise of God's saving acts for his people and for individuals. Descriptive praise (hymn) is the praise of God for his being and his activity as a whole. The Hebrew title of the Psalter, *tehillim,* indicates that the primary intention of the book as a whole is to render praise to God.[69]

God's steadfast love (*hesed*) points to his covenantal faithfulness. The hymn surveys the character and work of God in a general fashion and from further afield. The hymn developed with a variety of forms. The simplest kind is that exhibited in the shortest psalm, Ps. 117, which has two elements: 1) an imperative call to praise in v. 1, and 2) the reason for praising in v. 2:

> 1   Praise the Lord, all you nations!
>   Extol him, all you peoples
>
> 2   For great is his steadfast love towards us,
>   And the faithfulness of the Lord endures forever!

This basic pattern is followed in longer hymns, like Ps. 113 and 146, and in solo adaptations (Ps. 103 and 104). Other hymns double this pattern by repeating the pair of elements, such as Ps. 100 (vv. 1-2, 3-4, 5), 147, and 148. The Songs of Zion, notably Ps. 46, 48, 76, and 87, praise God as the Lord of Jerusalem and of temple worship. A number of the royal psalms, particularly Ps. 2, 21, 72, and 110, in focusing upon the Davidic king, were meant to honour God as the Lord of the Davidic covenant.[70]

---

[68]   Westermann, *Praise and Lament in the Psalms.*
[69]   Miller, *Interpreting the Psalms,* 67.
[70]   Allen, *Psalms,* 22.

2. Life Setting (*Sitz im Leben*)

Hymns belong to the social context of Israel's worship. They contain references to the temple and the sanctuary (Ps. 100:2, 4; 135:2); to the feasts, music, processions, and dancing; and to the presence of the congregation.

3. Structure

Declarative praise psalms (hymns) include Ps. 8, 19, 29, 33, 65-66, 100, 104-105, 111, 113-114, 117, 135-136, 145-146, and 148-150. Ordinarily, a hymn contains three elements:

a) An introductory call (invitation) sets the characteristic tone of praise. It consists of an exhortation or invitation extended by a leader to a group or a whole assembly (Ps. 33:1, 149:1) or to the whole world (Ps. 117:1) to praise God. On occasions the poet might call upon himself to do it (104:1). This element is sometimes absent in a hymn (19).

b) The body of the poem develops the motives for praise. It is usually introduced by *ki* (for, because). The reasons for praise include the various attributes or qualities of Yahweh and his deeds in history. Prominent among his qualities are his steadfast love (*hesed*) and everlasting faithfulness (*emet*). "For great is his steadfast love toward us, and the faithfulness of the Lord endures for ever" (117:2; cf. 136). Creation, for the Hebrews, is one of God's actions in history and for which Yahweh is to be praised. "You set the earth on its foundations . . . you cover it with the deep as with a garment; the waters stood above the mountains. At your rebuke they flee; at the sound of your thunder they take to flight . . . . You set a boundary that they may not pass, so that they might not again cover the earth" (Ps. 104:5-9; cf. 33:8-9). Israel's God is not only their creator, he is even more their

Saviour. Hence the theme of the exodus, deliverance, becomes an important motif of praise (114).[71]

c) A conclusion in the form of a renewed call or recapitulation of invitation to praise (Ps. 145:21). Not every hymn has this element.

117:1: Invitation to praise
2: Motives of praise

113 1-3: Call to praise
4-9: Body: the great God (4-6)
He helps the poor (7-9)

145:1-3: Call to praise
4-20: Body, praises the greatness and goodness of Yahweh
21: Renewed call to praise

i. Psalm 8: Divine Majesty and Human Dignity

1   O Lord, our Sovereign,
how majestic is your name in all the earth!
You have set your glory above the heavens.

2   Out of the mouths of babes and infants
you have founded a bulwark because of your foes,
to silence the enemy and the avenger.

3   When I look at your heaven the work of your fingers,
the moon and the stars that you have established;

4   what are human beings that you are mindful of them,

---

[71]   Raymond E. Brown, et al. *The New Jerome Biblical Commentary* (Bangalore: TPI, 1991), 525.

mortals that you care for them?

5   Yet you have made them a little lower than God,
    and crowned them with glory and honour.

6   You have given them dominion over the works of your hands;
    you have put all things under their feet,

7   all sheep and oxen,
    and also the beasts of the field,

8   the birds of the air, and the fish of the sea,
    whatever passes along the paths of the seas.

9   O LORD, our Sovereign,
    how majestic is your name in all the earth!

a.   Introduction

Ps. 8 is another articulation of creation faith. It is a canticle of praise to God. This hymn finds its parallel in the *Canticle of the Sun* and the *Canticle of the Creatures* sung by St. Francis. The *Canticle of the Sun* is a meditation by one who looks around and sees God's work in the sun and moon and stars and praises him for Brother Wind and Sister Water, Brother Fire, and our Sister Mother Earth, for those who forgive, for our Sister Death.[72] The theme of Ps. 8 is the frailty of human beings, contrasted with the majestic glory of God and the place that God has given to human beings in his creation. This psalm manages to hold together an exalted view of Yahweh's majesty and a high estimate of human beings. It is a hymn, not to a human being, but to God as creator through a human. The psalmist

---

[72]   Carlo Maria Martini, *What Am I that You Care for Me? Praying with the Psalms* (Collegeville, MN: Liturgical Press, 1990), 42.

contemplates the beauty of the heavens with representation and wonder, and he is led to exclaim, "How (*ma*) majestic is your name in all the earth" (8:1). The scene shifts, and his eyes turn to himself, and a disconcerting question arises in his mind: "What (*ma*) are human beings?" (8:4). It constitutes the specificity of this psalm. Yet whatever humans are, it is God's gift as well. "Human dignity in its entirety points to God who has given that dignity to man: 'Let him who boasts, boast of the Lord'" (1 Cor. 1:31; 2 Cor. 10:17).[73]

b. Structure

8:1a: Introductory refrain
1b-8: Body of the psalm
9: Concluding refrain

1-2: Communal praise

> 1a: Invocation
> 1a: Exclamation
> 1b-2: Direct praise

3-8: Hymn of the individual

> 3-4: Exclamation

5-6: Direct praise

> 7-8: List of subdued beings
> 9: Communal praise[74]

---

73 Weiser, *The Psalms*, 145.

74 Erhard S. Gerstenberger, *Psalms. Part 1 with an Introduction to Cultic Poetry*, Vol. XIV. *The Forms of the Old Testament Literature* (Grand Rapids, MI: Eerdmans, 1988), 67.

c. Interpretation

The psalm begins and ends with the same thought: the majesty of God. It is a Hebrew technique known as inclusion (or cyclic composition), whose purpose is to highlight the central theme in the piece. Though the thought in v. 9 is the same as v. 1a, still it is repeated with "a wider and more comprehensive meaning,"[75] because the body of the psalm demonstrates the veracity of v. 1a.

The phrase "O Lord Our Sovereign" (1a) is rendered differently in various Bibles. The New Jerusalem Bible uses "Yahweh Our Lord." The underlying reference is to God's lordship or dominion, which extends to the ends of the earth. Your name is another way of referring to God himself (cf. 68:4, 135:3, 97:12, 145:1-2).

The hymn proper has two unequal parts: 8:1b-2 and 3-8. 8:1b implies that the Lord is the ruler over the universe from a throne above the earth. It also gives insight into the psalmist's picture of the universe.[76] "Out of the mouths of babes and infants" (2): babes and infants would represent those on earth who see God's glory reflected in his creation and praise him for it. They could stand for the worshippers implied in the refrain; for simple, god-fearing religious people as opposed to the proud and the irreligious (foes, enemy, avenger); for the childlike attitude of human existence, which discovers the world, day by day, with a wonder and full of joy (a new Adam who names everything).

---

[75] Franz Delitzsch, "Psalms," Vol. 5 in *Commentary on the Old Testament*, eds. C. F. Keil and F. Delitzsch, Book 3 (Grand Rapids, MI: Eerdmans, 1980), 156.

[76] Jerome F. D. Creach, "Psalm 8. What Does It Mean to be Human?" in *Psalms: Interpretation. Bible Studies* (Louisville, KY: Westminster John Knox Press, 1998), 69; Walter Brueggemann, *The Message of the Psalms. A Theological Commentary.* Augsburg Old Testament Studies (Minneapolis: Augsburg, 1984), 36.

The "foes" (2) could be mythological figures (Ps. 74:13-14, 89:10) or giants (Gen. 6:4). "The enemy and the avenger" could refer to be variants of names for the dragon or chaos, otherwise known by different names such as Leviathan, Tannin, Rahab, Behemoth, Yamm, Mot, Marduk, and Apophis.[77] In this case, the "bulwark" would be the firmament that blocks off the rebels from the celestial sphere. It is more likely that the reference is to the human enemies of God, who neither accept him nor submit to him (cf. Ps. 28:5, 74:22). The praise of the religious people would then constitute the bulwark. It would reduce to silence the clamor of the proud and mighty who exert themselves against God. The contrast between the attitude of praise and that of rebellion is a great intuition of this psalm (cf. 1 Cor. 1:27).

"The work of your fingers" (3): The heavens are the work of his hands. The vision of the heavenly brilliance arouses in him the thought of the creator of all splendor. His wisdom is manifested in beauty and intricate pattern of the start (cf. 136:5). He has arranged the stars with the work of his fingers. In contrast to the "arm" of the Lord ("Power," 89:10), the "fingers" or hands would designate both the supreme ease with which God created and also the wonderful beauty and order of his design. The above expression is evidence of the artisan character of creation. It is not merely an act of the intellect from a distance, but an act that requires delicateness and tenderness.

From v. 4 onward, the poem moves on to the thought of God's great goodness and love toward humans, his insignificant creatures: "What are human beings?" The rest of the psalm, excluding the concluding refrain, dwells on God's wonderful care for humans. The present verse is a fine example of synonymous parallelism. Hence "human beings" (*enosh,* man, to be in poor health) are "mortals" (*ben adam,* son of man) taken from the

---

77 Crenshaw, *The Psalms,* 62.

earth *(adama)* and consequently mortals. A human is a fine creature, one made of dust, who returns to dust eventually (Gen. 3:19). How do such beings deserve God's loving remembrance and care?

Verse 4 can be paraphrased as, "What is so special about these puny creatures that you would pay attention to them?" The intended answer would seem to be, "Nothing." Compared to God, humans have nothing to boast about; they are limited in knowledge and ability, and in the end they are swallowed up in the ground from which they came.[78]

The answer to this question as well as to the interrogative "What are human beings?" is found in v. 5. A child of Adam is made by his creator as "little lower than God." "Little lower than" signifies "to be short of, wanting in something, to deprive anyone of something."[79] A human being is defined by subtraction. But this "little" is decisive: he is "little less than a god" (NJB, RSV). This confusion is due to the plural form of *Elohim,* which can stand for God, gods, or angels. The more correct rendering would be "little less than angels" because, in the OT, God is God and humans are humans. Secondly, the psalm stresses very much the greatness of the God who makes man in his own image and likeness (Gen. 1:26-28); it stands for his dominion over plants and animals. Hence humans are little less than God only in the aspect of dominion, not in other aspects.

Though human beings are insignificant, still God has crowned them through a symbolic investiture (5b). God has given them dominion over all his works and put everything under their feet (6). Human beings have "dominion over the works of your hands," that is, the animals, both domestic and wild, and the

---

[78]   Creach, *Psalms,* 70.
[79]   Delitzsch, *Psalms,* 153.

birds of the air and the creatures in the seas. Verses 7-8 give us an enumeration of all the subjects over which humans are the rulers. Ps. 8:3-8 is reminiscent of other passages of scripture like Ps. 115:16 and Gen. 1:26-28, 2:19-20.

What are human beings? They are the images of God. As such they have power but they are not the masters. They possess glory, but it is received. They occupy a unique place in creation but, at the same time, it is one that has been assigned to them.

Patrick Coughlan is right when he sums up the whole poem as follows: "The psalm is a very unified one with one central dominating theme—the greatness, power, wisdom, and goodness of God the Creator. In the section which speaks of man (vv. 4-8) the whole emphasis is on the goodness of God to man, what God has done for man, not on the greatness of man as such."[80]

d. Christian Transposition

The first line of reading the psalm is anthropological, that is, with humanity at the center; the second is Christological, and the third eucharistic. The Christological reading of this psalm is suggested by certain passages in the NT, like Heb. 1 and 1 Cor. 15. Do I acknowledge Christ, Lord of life and history? Is the eucharistic Christ the center of the life of the church?[81]

Can we state, without any reserve, that human beings are really the masters of the earth, as implied in the psalm? The humans we see around us appear to be quite different. They have little dignity to their credit and very little under their dominion.

---

[80] P. Coughlan, "Praising God in the Psalms," *Clergy Review* 63 (1978): 375.

[81] Martini, *What Am I*, 45-47.

In the incarnated person of Jesus, however, all the idealism of the psalm becomes a reality, as pointed out by the letter to the Hebrews (2:5-9). One can sing and pray it of this Son of man, without corrections or reserve. He is one who attained the fullness of humanity (Eph. 4:13). God has put all things in subjection under his feet (1 Cor. 15:27, Eph. 1:22).

Christians who have received the spirit of sonship (Gal 4:5) participate in the authentic dignity of humans. What are human beings? They are the younger brothers and sisters and images of Jesus Christ. What are sons and daughters? Sons and daughters of God. "Glorify God in your body" (1 Cor. 6:20). "Truly I tell you, just as you did it to one of the least of these who are members of my family, you did it to me" (Mt. 25:40). "It is no longer I who live, but it is Christ who lives in me" (Gal. 2:20). "What are human beings" (Job 7:17-21).

Hebrews 2:5-9 mentions Ps. 8:4. Hebrews holds up a portrait of what humanity is intended to be. The intention of God for every person is Christ. Hebrews 2:8 states, "We do not yet see everything in subjection to them [humans]," but (v. 9) "we do not see Jesus." Jesus gives the example where dominion did not, and will not, become dominion. When all things are finally put under his feet, then all will see creation cared for in the way God intends.[82]

ii. Psalm 19: God's Glory in Nature and in the Law

1 The heavens are telling the Glory of God;
and the firmament proclaims his handiwork.

2 Day to day pours forth speech,
and night to night declares knowledge.

82 Creach, *Psalms*, 75-76.

3   There is no speech, nor are there words;
    their voice is not heard;

4   yet their voice goes out through all the earth,
    and their words to the end of the world.
    In the heavens he has set a tent for the sun,

5   which comes out like a bridegroom from his wedding canopy.
    and like a strong man runs its course with joy.

6   Its rising is from the end of the heavens,
    and its circuit to the end of them;
    and nothing is hid from its heat.

7   The law of the LORD is perfect, reviving the soul;
    the decrees of the LORD are sure, making wise the simple;

8   the precepts of the LORD are right,
    rejoicing the heart;
    the commandment of the LORD is clear,
    enlightening the eyes;

9   the fear of the LORD is pure,
    enduring forever;
    the ordinances of the LORD are true
    and righteous altogether.

10 More to be desired are they than gold,
    even much fine gold;
    sweeter also than honey,
    and drippings of the honeycomb.

11 Moreover by them is your servant warned;
    in keeping them there is great reward.

12 But who can detect their errors?
clear me from hidden faults.

13 Keep back your servant also from the insolent;
do not let them have dominion over me.
Then I shall be blameless,
and innocent of great transgression.

14 Let the words of my mouth and the meditation of my heart
be acceptable to you,
O LORD, my rock and my redeemer.

a. Introduction

There is a relationship between Ps. 18:20-32 and Ps. 19:7-13.[83]
Ps. 19 starts with praise of God's majesty: "I take this to be the
greatest poem in the Psalter and one of the greatest lyrics in the
world."[84] Nevertheless, doubts as to the unity of this beautiful
poem have been voiced by many. The reasons for this are the
following: 1) The presence of radically different themes in 19:1-6
(a psalm of descriptive praise) and 7-14 (a wisdom psalm); 2)
the remarkable change in style: vv. 2-6 are vibrant while 7-14
appear monotonous; 3) the first section presupposes a mythical
mentality in comparison with the legalism of the second; and 4)
the presence of differing titles for God; *el* in the first and *Yahweh*
in the second.[85] Ps. 19 is held by some scholars as one unit.[86]

---

83 See Farmer, *International Bible Commentary*, 852-853.
84 C. S. Lewis, *Reflections*, 56.
85 See Weiser, *The Psalms*, 197; Gerstenberger, *Psalms*, 101; Farmer,
Bible Commentary, 852.
86 Farmer, *International Bible Commentary*, 853; Keck et al., *NIB*, Vol.
4, 751; Weiser, *The Psalms*, 197; Terrien, *The Psalms*, 208.

It is possible to view the psalm as a unified whole. In its final form, this psalm is not an "either-or" but a "both-and." As Helmer Ringgren says, "The heavens that tell the glory of God and the firmament that proclaims his handiwork, on the one hand, and God's law that revives the soul, on the other, are actually two manifestations of one and the same divine will."[87] A change of style is understandable with a change of theme. The sun could serve as the hinge uniting the two sections, as the *Torah* (law) can also emit light. With Franz Delitzsch, we could say that Ps. 19 "celebrates God's revelation of himself in nature and in the Law."[88]

There are some, however, who prefer to treat the psalm as two separate ones: 19:1-6 as a nature psalm and 19:7-14 as a wisdom psalm.[89] Nonetheless, what is bequeathed to us in the Bible is one psalm. A. F. Kirkpatrick says that God has two great volumes in which he reveals himself: nature and scripture. The first section deals with God's revelation of himself in nature; the second deals with the revelation of himself in the law.[90]

b. Structure

1-4a: Hymn to creation
1-4b: Hymn to the heavens
4c-6: Hymn to the sun
7-10: Hymn to the *Torah*
11-14: Petition

[87] Helmer Ringgren, *The Faith of the Psalmists* (London: Fortress, 1963), 104-105.
[88] Delitzsch, *Psalms*, 279.
[89] William Barclay, *The Lord Is My Shepherd. Expositions of Selected Psalms* (Glasgow, Scotland: William Collins Sons, 1980), 96.
[90] Ibid., 97.

11-12a: Confession of sin
12b-13b: Petition
13c-d: Affirmation of confidence
14: Plea to be heard[91]

c. Interpretation

1-4b: Song in Praise of Creation

Creation must have been conceived of as participating in exalting and praising God's glory. As Weiser rightly stresses, the poet "tunes his contemplation of Nature right from the outset to a religious keynote."[92] It is the key to the true understanding of the first part of the psalm. The whole of nature is at God's service to sing the praise of God and to be the vehicle of his revelation. "The heavens and the firmament" are personified. According to the Hebrew understanding, they consist of many layers. They are also the frontier to the celestial world. "God" *(el)* stands for the God of power, the creator.

"Day/night" (v. 2) are also personifications. They serve as a vehicle of revelation that is passed on in an unbroken tradition.

"There is no speech . . . yet their voice goes out through all the earth" (vv. 3-4). Nature possesses an inherent power of communication, a communication that transcends the barriers of spoken language. It is a universal language. "The heavens are

---

[91]   Gerstenberger, *Psalms,* 100; see also Farmer, *International Bible Commentary,* 853; Brown et al., *The New Jerome,* 529; Keck et al., *NIB,* Vol. 4, 751.

[92]   Weiser, *The Psalms,* 198.

the book from which the whole world can derive its knowledge of God!"[93]

4c-6: Hymn in Praise of the Sun

This section introduces a great protagonist, the sun, pictured as a bridegroom who comes forth out of a bridal canopy (*huppah:* the ritual canopy under which a bride and bridegroom were married). What is presupposed here is the mythological idea that the sun-god rests during the night in the sea, lying in the arms of his mistress.[94] Unlike in Eccl 1:5, the sun performs his role *with joy*. Evidently he is not the God of the Israelites. Instead it is God who set a tent for the sun.[95] "Nothing is hid from" everything. To some, the sun is the "voice" (v. 4) that goes out through all the earth.[96] To others, the action of the sun (i.e., emitting heat) repeats or translates the universal message of the heavens and the firmament.[97] "This science is man's attempt to decipher the mysterious writing, exhibited by nature, which God's finger has engraved there for all to read, that his power and his wisdom may be proclaimed."[98]

7-10: Praise of the Lord

In form and content, Ps. 19:7-14 bears analogy to Ps. 119. Ps. 19:7-14 proves to be the earlier model, since it is clearly divided into a hymn in praise of the law (vv. 7-10) and a personal prayer of supplication (vv. 11-14). In respect of the predominance of form over subject matter in vv. 7-10, the psalm is quite surpassed

[93] Ibid., 199; Barclay, *The Lord Is My Shepherd*, 103-106.
[94] Weiser, *The Psalms*, 199.
[95] See Keck et al., *NIB*, Vol. 4, 752.
[96] See D. Cox, *The Psalms in the Life of God's People*, 57.
[97] L. Alonso Schokel, *Trenta Salmi: Poesia e Preghiera*. Studi Biblici (Bologna: EDB, 1982): 98.
[98] Weiser, *The Psalms*, 200.

by Ps. 119.[99] A. T. Kirkpatrick makes mention of "God's two great volume of nature and the scriptures."[100] In this section, we have before us the second volume that contains the revelation of God in the law. Originally, the word "*Torah*" did not signify "law" in the sense of a postexilic written document. It referred to oral prescriptions, prohibitions, and statutes of moral jurisprudence, transmitted by parents to children from generation to generation (Prov. 1:8, 3:1, 4:2, 5:20). It may also have designated the teaching by popular or court sages (Ps. 78:1; Prov. 13:14, 28:4, 29:8, 31:25). It could also have referred to the education of human beings directed by Yahweh himself or by his prophets (Job 22:22, Isa. 30:9, Jer. 8:8). The word "*Torah*" is etymologically related to *moreh,* the autumnal rain that revives the greenness of vegetation after the estival drought, or the master in pedagogical circles or schools.[101] The *Torah,* instruction, the focus of vv. 7-10, is a pointing out, an all-encompassing law as we today understand it. It is the greatest gift that God could have given to his people, a gift that revealed to them his will. Hence, characteristic peculiarities attributed to the law are the peculiarities of the God who is behind it. So in praising it, the poet is praising God himself.[102]

The law of the Lord is "perfect" (v. 7): spotless, harmless, directed toward one's well-being; "reviving the soul": imparting newness of life. "The decrees of the Lord" (cf. Ex. 31:18, 32:15) are a corroborative and instructive attestation. They are "sure" in the sense that the law is raised above all doubt. The "Precepts" (v. 8) stand for the various injunctions about one's obligations. These are "right": straight or upright. The commandment of the Lord is "clear, enlightening the eyes," enlightening one's

---

[99]   Ibid., 2001.
[100] A. T. Kirkpatrick, *The Book of Psalms,* 101.
[101] Terrien, *The Psalms,* 211.
[102] Weiser, *The Psalms,* 202.

Mathew V. Thekkekara SDB

understanding, even one's whole condition (cf. Prov. 6:23). "The fear of the Lord" (v. 9) is reverence in the sense of respect and awe. It is what God's revelation demands, effects, and maintains. The fear of the Lord is the beginning of wisdom (Ps. 111:10; Prov. 1:7, 9:10). It is *pure*, clean, without dross. The ordinances of the Lord are "righteous" in the sense that they are right and appropriate (cf. Deut. 4:8).[103] The personal name for Yahweh (Lord) occurs six times in vv. 7-9. What makes life possible is relatedness to God, and this personal relatedness is mediated by the *Torah*.[104] The *Torah* is to be desired more than "gold" and it is sweeter than "honey" (v. 10). It is like the most precious treasure that one could possess and like the tastiest food that one could delight in.

The law is the complete revelation of the will of God. It is the revelation of the full life God wants us to live, and the guidance and the inspiration to live it. The law is God's testimony to himself and to human beings. It never fails and is absolutely trustworthy and completely stable. It is such that even the simple person can live well, if that person will take it as the guide and director of life.[105]

11-14: Prayer of the Psalmist

Learning the law was sweeter than honey and more precious than gold. But "moreover" (v. 11) introduces a paradox. The psalmist realises that the law is perfect, but he is not; it illumines him, still some things escape him; it is appreciated and liked by him, but he is unable to fulfill it. So he is induced to make a confession of his errors (vv. 12-13), actions out of ignorance, "hidden faults" (unconscious deeds) and "insolent faults" (rebellion against

---

103 Terrien, *The Psalms*, 212-213.
104 Keck et al., *NIB*, Vol. 4, 752.
105 Barclay, *The Lord Is My Shepherd*, 112-113.

the divine authority or deliberate defiance of God). Already absolved, he completes his prayer, full of confidence in the Lord, his "rock," symbol of security and defence, and his "redeemer" (his *goèl*) (v. 14), his nearest kin (by covenant) who will vindicate him. The God who set the sun on its course is the same God the psalmist has experienced personally as "my next of kin"!

Ps. 19:1-6 praises Yahweh's expressed will. In 19:7-10, Yahweh's *Torah* sustains our life. The one who prays has personally experienced the beneficial effects of the divine *Torah* (19:11-14).[106]

We could sum up the movement of Ps. 19 briefly in the words of Delitzsch: "The Poet begins with the praise of the glory of God the Creator, and rises from this to the praise of the mercy of God the Lawgiver; and thus through the praise, springing from wondering and loving adoration, he clears the way to the prayer for justification and sanctification."[107]

d. Christian Transposition

The following are some pointers that could aid someone praying this psalm:

1) The light of Jesus' resurrection illuminates the symbolic structure of creation. A Christian contemplates a creation that is partly restored by Christ and one that awaits to be restored partly. This leads one to have the right view of ecology.
2) Christ can be viewed as the sun of righteousness and the bridegroom.

---

[106] See Farmer, *International Bible Commentary*, 853.
[107] Delitzch, *Psalms*, 280.

3) A meditation on the law could lead to a contemplation of the law of the Spirit and raising a lot of love for church law, canon law.
4) Rom. 7:14-25 could be viewed as prolongation and clarification of Ps. 19:11-14.

iii. Psalm 29: Yahweh's Self-Disclosure in a Storm

1 Ascribe to the LORD, O Heavenly beings,
ascribe to the LORD glory and strength.

2 Ascribe to the LORD the glory of his name;
worship the LORD in holy splendor.

3 The voice of the LORD is over the waters;
the God of glory thunders,
the LORD, over mighty waters.

4 The voice of the LORD is powerful;
the voice of the LORD is full of majesty.

5 The voice of the LORD breaks the cedars;
the Lord breaks the cedars of Lebanon.

6 He makes Lebanon skip like a calf,
and Sirion like a young wild ox.

7 The voice of the LORD flashes forth flames of fire.

8 The Voice of the LORD shakes the wilderness;
the Lord shakes the wilderness of Kadesh.

9 The voice of the LORD causes the oaks to whirl,
and strips the forest bare;
and in his temple all say, "Glory!"

10 The LORD sits enthroned over the flood;
   the Lord sits enthroned as king forever.

11 May the LORD give strength to his people!
   May the LORD bless his people with peace!

a. Introduction

Ps. 29 is probably the oldest psalm.[108] Important lexemes link Ps. 29 to Ps. 28.[109] This is a hymn in praise of the towering majesty of Yahweh. Unlike Ps. 8 or Ps. 19, herein one finds the greatness, power, and glory of God revealed in the fury of a storm. Its exquisite poetical beauty and vigorous power are noteworthy.

Ps. 29 is, probably, an adaptation of an original Canaanite poetic hymn in praise of the storm-god Baal. It is an important example of how the people of God appreciated poems and sacred songs even of other cultures.[110] For the Jews, anything borrowed is to be reinterpreted according to their outlook and religion. Consequently it is in praise of Yahweh, the Lord of creation and victor over the forces of chaos.

Underlying this song is also the idea of the numinous, the awe-inspiring majesty of God filling human heart with fear and trembling, on the one hand, and attraction, on the other. "In this song the polarity and tension of faith, welding into a unity man's fear and trembling as well as his exultation and rapture at the presence of God, is expressed in a manner which form the

---

108 Martini, *What Am I,* 60; Keck et al., *NIB,* Vol. 4, 792.
109 Farmer, *International Bible Commentary,* 864.
110 Craghan, *Psalms,* 19; Martini, *What Am I,* 60; Brueggemann, *The Message,* 142; Farmer, *International Bible Commentary,* 865.

artistic point of view is just as original as it is appropriate to its subject."[111]

b. Structure

Superscription

> 1-2: Invitation to glorify God
> 3-9: Description of Yahweh's power
> 10-11: Praise of Yahweh[112]

c. Interpretation

29:1-2: Invitation to Glorify God

The storm raging on earth is sandwiched between two lofty scenes in heaven (vv. 1-2 and 10-11). In vv. 1-2, as Weiser beautifully puts it, "the poet has composed a powerful overture for his hymn."[113] This overture is, at the same time, in the form of a synthetic or repetitive parallelism. "Ascribe": give; in the original, it is a verbalised exclamation or interjection: "Come on!" "Be ready!" "Lord" *(Yahweh)* appears eighteen times in eleven verses.[114] The totally God-centered character of the psalm is evidenced by it. "Heavenly beings" *(bene elim:* sons of the gods) are the ones who constitute Yahweh's court and act as his messengers and emissaries (cf. Ps. 89:6).[115]

---

[111] Weiser, *The Psalms,* 260.
[112] Gerstenberger, *Psalms,* 130; Farmer, *International Bible Commentary,* 864.
[113] Weiser, *The Psalms,* 262.
[114] Farmer, *International Bible Commentary,* 864-865; Keck et al., *NIB,* Vol. 4, 792.
[115] Terrien, *The Psalms,* 276.

"Glory" (*kabod*) refers to a spectacular self-manifestation of God in history. His glory fills the whole earth (Isa. 6:3). It is made known through the signs he worked in Egypt and in the wilderness (Num. 14:22-23). In our hymn, there is a spectacular revelation of his glory in a storm, and the celestial choirs react to it. "The glory of his name" is the glory to his name, which is equivalent to his august person. "Worship": adore; the Hebrew verb used here means "to bow down, prostrate oneself" (cf. 2 Sam. 14:33; 1 Kgs 1:23). The NRSV version uses "In holy splendor," and the LXX translates it as "holy court." But this requires a slight modification in the Hebrew version. The more commonly held form is "in holy splendor," that is, wearing special vestments for this unique occasion. Basing oneself on the linguistic evidence from the Ugaritic, two other renderings are possible: "in the revelation of the Holy one" or "when the Holy one makes his appearance."[116]

29:3-9: Description of the Storm

Ps. 29:3-9 is a poetic description of a thunderstorm, usually attributed by the Canaanites to Baal. This psalm is fundamentally polemical, for it clearly attributes all power to Yahweh (Lord), who is enthroned in v. 9 with the exclamation, "Glory!" That enthronement is indeed the effect of v. 9 is indicated by the affirmation of Yahweh's kingship in v. 10, followed by the appeal for Yahweh to fulfill the royal role of blessing the people.[117] "The Voice (*qol*) of the Lord" (v. 3) occurs seven times in the body of the psalm, like successive peals of thunder. The "voice," in this context, is equated with the person of Yahweh.[118] It is

---

116 K. Luke, *Israel before Yahweh: An Exposition of Selected Psalms* (Quilon: Assisi Press, 1978), 49.

117 Keck et al., *NIB*, Vol. 4, 792.

118 Martini, *What Am I*, 60; Brown et al., *The New Jerome Biblical Commentary*, 531; Keck et al., *NIB*, Vol. 4, 792.

upon the "waters," which probably refers to the waves of the Mediterranean Sea. "Mighty waters" would refer to "torrential" or "immensity" of waters. The poet's vision of the sea would have evoked in his mind recollections of the primordial chaos and God's victory over it. The voice of Yahweh is might and majesty itself (v. 4). "Lord" (*Yahweh*) is mentioned eighteen times in this psalm. So it is filled with the name of God, who is present and who saves.[119]

There is a song of new orientation in verses 3-9a, which present the chaos (cosmic disorientation) in which this God has been at work to conquer. The narrative characterises a great rainstorm that sweeps off the Mediterranean Sea (v. 3) through Lebanon (vv. 5-6) and on to the southern desert (vv. 7-8).[120] The voice of the Lord continually reduces to smithereens even "cedars" (v. 5), which are paragons of height, strength, and majesty. "Lebanon" and "Sirion" (v. 6) could be understood either in a geographic sense or, more rightly, as a symbolic allusion to the mysterious regions of the north (abode of the god?). Verse 7 would imply that his voice emits flashes of lightning. The "wilderness" (v. 8) denotes regions without permanent settlements or nomadic areas. As Kadesh appears in Ugaritic texts in connection with Lebanon and Sirion, it designates the northern region and not the Sinai area, as traditionally held by people. The breaking of cedars, the flames of fire, the convulsing earth, and the tireless come together to provide an image of power.

The consequence of the storm is described in v. 9. Some would even translate it as "The voice of the Lord makes the hinds to calve, and the mountain goats to calve before time." Such a version is possible with slight modifications in the original. It very realistically describes the terror created by the storm. The

---

119   Martini, *What Am I*, 60.
120   Brueggemann, *The Message*, 142.

NRSV rendition is more in agreement with the Masoretic Text. This verse ends with the heavenly beings raising the praise of Yahweh. "That which the poet, in vv. 1-2, has called them to do, now takes place. Yahweh receives back His glory, which is imminent in the universe, in the thousand-voiced echo of adoration."[121] "In his temple all say 'Glory!'" (v. 9), intending it as a hymn in praise of the august majesty of God. This verse is "the key verse of the whole psalm—it leads us away from the commotions on the earth up to the heavenly sanctuary where the company of the heavenly beings recognises and glorifies these very occurrences on the earth as a revelation of glory of Yahweh."[122] The temple is Yahweh's palace in heaven. The "all" stands for the whole of creation, which the poet has personified and represented as a group of pious and fervent believers assembled together to sing the divine praises. "Peace" (v. 11) is not merely the cessation of hostilities but the condition of wholeness whereby living becomes celebration. "Peace" (*shalom*) is total well-being.

29:10-11: Conclusion

In Ps. 29, Yahweh is the Lord of the storm, and because of his victory over chaos, he sits enthroned forever in sublime imperturbability over the flood, above the waters. His people, Israel, enjoy the benefits of his triumph. He bestows on them the gifts of strength that is equivalent to salvation and peace (*shalom*), the total well-being of Israel. The psalm proclaims the power of the voice of God, whose word has created all things, in nature, in the history of peoples, in the life of Christ, and in the lives of each one of us, and invites us to see the world and human existence as supported and animated by that word.[123] Delitzsch

---

[121] Delitzsch, *Psalms*, 372.
[122] von Rad, *Old Testament Theology*, 360.
[123] Martini, *What Am I*, 62.

sums up the psalm beautifully: "*Gloria in excelsis* is its beginning and *pax in terris* its conclusion."[124]

d. The Christian Transposition

The brute force of the storm is itself a revelation of God. He is the Lord of the storm and, consequently to him, to him alone belong glory, dominion, power and majesty. The Lord's voice that is heard above the storm is also creative and salvific, extending the blessings of salvation to all. All are to react to this and cry: "To him be glory forever, Amen."

The NT presents Christ as the master of the tempest (Mt. 8:23-27). Again, Matthew describes the death of Jesus in terms of theophany.

How do we receive the gift of peace? What do I do for peace? What is actually done in my community, or nation, to create the atmosphere of reconciliation in our daily relationships? *Shalom* (peace, well-being, security) does not begin with our efforts but with our openness to God's claim upon us and the ways God has gifted us. "Psalm 29 becomes a call to yield control to the sovereignty of God. Enduring strength and *shalom* will derive from joining the heavenly beings in their cry, 'Glory!' (v. 9c). To paraphrase the first answer in the Westminster Shorter Catechism, the chief end of humankind is to glorify God and enjoy God for ever."[125]

"Epiphany follows Christmas; Psalm 29 spans the two seasons. The movement of Psalm 29 from proclaiming God's glory (v. 9c) to peace on earth (v. 11) recalls the account of Jesus' birth in

---

[124] Delitzsch, *Psalms,* 373.
[125] Keck et al., *NIB,* Vol. 4, 793.

Luke (Luke 2:14). The birth of Jesus is the event by which God's universal reign became manifest."[126]

iv. Psalm 114: God's Wonders at the Exodus (cf. Ex. 14:1-31)

1   When Israel went out from Egypt,
    the house of Jacob from a people of strange language,

2   Judah became God's sanctuary,
    Israel his dominion.

3   The sea looked and fled;
    Jordan turned back.

4   The mountains skipped like rams,
    the hills like lambs.

5   Why is it, O sea, that you fled?
    O Jordan, that you turn back?

6   O mountains, that you skip like rams?
    O hills, like lambs?

7   Tremble, O earth, at the presence of the Lord,
    at the presence of the God of Jacob,

8   who turns the rock into a pool of water,
    the flint into a spring of water.

---

[126]   Ibid., 794.

a. Introduction

In the LXX and Vulgate, Ps. 114 and 115 form a single composition (Ps. 113a and b), but the two psalms are independent literary units.[127] Ps. 114 is second of the Egyptian Hallel (113-118). It is the praise of God, who has delivered his people from Egypt and brought them into the Promised Land.[128] "Ps. 114 is a historical poem, describing the transformation of nature at the exodus (v. 1, 3, 4), and affirming that it was due to the presence of the God of Jacob."[129] The psalm was regarded as a Passover hymn[130] that was sung in the liturgy appointed for the eighth day of that festival.[131] The reference to the Kingship of God and to his epiphany (vv. 2, 7) points rather to the Covenant Festival of Yahweh. Probably its transfer to the Feast of Passover took place in the late pre-exilic or post-exilic period. It is a hymn in praise of the God who chose the people as "his sanctuary," a decision that represents the fundamental saving fact of the cult of the Covenant Festival. Since the two kingdoms of Judah and Israel are mentioned side by side (v. 2), the psalm seems to date back to the time before the downfall of the Northern Kingdom (721 BC). It consists of four symmetrically constructed strophes: 1-2, 3-4, 5-6, and 7-8.[132] This psalmodic sketch about the exodus and the crossing of the Jordan affects a theatrical swiftness and an almost humourous apostrophe

---

[127] Leopold Sabourin, *The Psalms. Their Origin and Meaning* (Bangalore: TPI, 1971), 203; Farmer, *International Bible Commentary*, 906.

[128] See A. A. Anderson, *Psalms*. New Century Bible. Mathew Black and R. E. Clements, eds. (London: Oliphants, 1977), 782-783; McCann Jr., "The Book of Psalms," 1141.

[129] C. A. Briggs and E. G. Briggs, *The Book of Psalms*. The International Critical Commentary. S. R. Driver et al., eds. (Edinburgh: T. & T. Clark, 1969), 390.

[130] Allen, *Psalms 101-150*, 104; Delitzsch, *Psalms*, 207.

[131] Sabourin, *The Psalms*, 202.

[132] Weiser, *The Psalms*, 709.

to the elements of nature. The sketch is anchored on the fabulous "events" or "legends" of divine acts of marvels, bringing together the exodus itself with the turning around of the River Jordan and the piercing of the rock in the desert, horrors of waterless wastes.[133] The tone of the poem is exuberant, almost playful. The psalm is composed to build suspense over the meaning of what it tells about until the suspense is resolved at the conclusion.

b. Structure

1-2: The exodus and the birth of the nation
3-4: The miracles accompanying the exodus
5-6: Satirical humour
7-8: Submission before the Sovereign[134]

The poem's structure is chiastic:

A (vv. 1-2)
B (vv. 3-4)
B' (vv. 5-6)
A' (vv. 7-8)[135]

c. Interpretation

The Exodus and the Birth of the Nation (vv. 1-2)

The psalm begins with the account of the election of the people of Israel at the exodus from Egypt. The departure from

---

133 Terrien, *The Psalms,* 767.
134 Weiser, *The Psalms,* 709-712; Terrien, *The Psalms,* 769; McCann Jr., "The Book of Psalms," 1141.
135 Brown et al., eds., *The New Jerome Biblical Commentary,* 546.

Egypt and the settlement in the land mark its beginning and its conclusion (vv. 1-2). At the emergence of the people as a nation, history and *Heilsgeschichte* (drama of salvation) synchronise. By this means, the past becomes the present. This view rests on the belief that God and his action are always present, while humans in their inevitable temporality cannot grasp this present-ness except by "re-presenting" the action of God over and over again in his worship.[136] The exodus from Egypt is essentially the saving act of the God who helped his people and had compassion on their affliction. That they did not know the Egyptian language increased their burden from the oppressors. V. 1 also expresses the pride of a people who are conscious of their own character and have gained their freedom. Their *Heilsgeschichte* begins in this way: "Judah became his sanctuary and Israel his dominion." As God holds sway in both these states, their spiritual unity is both given and demanded. The psalm reflects the tradition of "greater Israel" and the theology of the cult of the covenant. God's *Heilsgeschichte* of the history of Israel lies in the fact that the people of Israel as a whole are a people holy to Yahweh. The psalmist speaks openly of Yahweh only in v. 7.[137]

As foreign languages are generally considered evil or that of a hostile nation, the Israelites mention that the Egyptians speak another language. "Israel" in v. 1a refers to the "greater Israel," the whole family of Jacob or the twelve-tribe league, and in v. 2b "Israel" is being differentiated from "Judah." This implies that the "sanctuary," the temple of Zion, and "dominion" (v. 2b) for Israel in general, the "house" of Jacob. The exodus has multiple meanings: deliverance from slavery, freedom from the adoration of the forces of nature personified as deities, and preparation for the covenant on Mount Sinai.[138]

---

[136]   Anderson, *Psalms*, 785.
[137]   Weiser, *The Psalms*, 709-710.
[138]   Terrien, *The Psalms*, 768; Delitzsch, *Psalms*, 207.

The Miracles Accompanying the Exodus (vv. 3-4)

The poet describes the nature miracles connected with the exodus. Nature and history are viewed as pointing to the sovereign power of the One God, who is the Lord of both. The dread of the terrible majesty of God causes the sea to flee from him, the Jordan to turn back, and the hills to tremble. The poet mentioning the receding of the sea on the occasion of the deliverance at the Red Sea (Ex. 14:21f.) becomes for him a flight from God as he draws near, and he changes the tradition of Joshua (3:14ff.) that the Jordan stood "still" into a turning back of the river. Again he depicts the quaking of the mountain at the revelation of God at Sinai (Ex. 19:16ff.), as in Ps. 29:6, with the grotesque word picture of rams and lambs skipping on the pasture. The same vitality of faith is expressed in the fact that the psalmist discerns in the miracles the response of nature and in this way becomes a visible witness to and interpreter of the divine epiphany.[139] "The dividing of the sea opens, and the dividing of the Jordan closes, the journey through the desert to Canaan."[140]

The Satirical Humour (vv. 5-6)

The poet asks the sea, the River Jordan, and the mountains why they behave so strangely. To the eye of faith, history is not something dead but something alive and dynamic. For in everything that comes to pass in history, faith encounters the God who is working in it and through it. The purpose of his questions is not only to indicate participation in the past as if it were present, but also to allow time for further reflection. At the same time, these questions exhibit a real touch of humour and

---

[139] Weiser, *The Psalms*, 710-711; Terrien, *The Psalms*, 769; Mays, *Psalms*, 363.

[140] Delitzsch, *Psalms*, 207.

irony, expressing freedom and spiritual superiority of a human being who, by virtue of his faith, unreservedly gives himself up to joy in God's sublime nature and sides with him in his bold dealings with nature.[141]

In this section, four elements are named: sea, Jordan River, mountains, hills. The water (sea and Jordan) is represented as an enemy of Yahweh. Mountains and hills reveal that exodus event is so momentous that even the fixtures of the cosmos are unfixed. The teller of the story wonders why the sea is such a coward and why the river is unable to stay in its place. So there is a contrast between Yahweh and the elements of creation. Now the humble God is exalted, and the exalted elements are humiliated.[142]

Submission before the Sovereign (vv. 7-8)

"Tremble, O earth, at the presence of the Lord." Thus he gives his answer: Nature will surely have good reason to be terrified at the appearing of him who is the Lord. For it is the glory of God which is exalted in this way by his creation at his epiphany. He calls upon the whole earth to tremble at the presence of the Lord and to give to the God of Jacob the honour that is his due. The psalmist may call this mighty God the God of his own people and see him at work in the history of the nation as a merciful Deliverer. He speaks not only of the water which flowed from the rock to quench the thirst of the people, but of the rock which became "a pool of water" and of the solid 'flint' which was turned 'into a spring of water.' The greatness of the miracle is a measure of the greatness not only of the transcendent majesty of the divine Lord, but also of his incomprehensible grace.[143]

---

[141] Weiser, *The Psalms,* 711-712.

[142] Brueggemann, *The Message,* 141.

[143] See Weiser, *The Psalms,* 712-713; Farmer, *International Bible Commentary,* 906.

"The presence," the 'face' of the cosmic master is immediately identified as "the God of Jacob" and the linking of the "house of Jacob" (v. 1) with the "God of Jacob" brings a climactic thrust to the entire psalm. "The causing of water to gush forth out of the flinty rock is a practical proof of unlimited omnipotence and of the grace which converts death into life."[144]

d. Christian Transposition

1. There is a light touch in the psalm that leads us to meditations on the proper relationship between the Lord and nature. The God who rules the cosmos is made known in space and time for the purpose of properly ordering the world and the human community.
2. The universe bows before the face of God. The early Christians perceived the cosmic God at work in quite ordinary events, like the birth of a child, as well as scandalously concrete events, like the cross.
3. "The church has read and sung the psalm in the light of what happened in Judah and Israel through Jesus Christ. It sees in his death and resurrection yet another and a climatic theophany of the divine rule in which the Presence assumes a new relation to people and place."[145]

v. Psalm 148: The Universal Praise of Yahweh

1 Praise the Lord!
   Praise the Lord from the heavens;
   Praise him in the heights!

---

144 Delitzsch, *Psalms*, 209.
145 Mays, *Psalms*, 365.

2   Praise him, all his angels;
    praise him, all his host!

3   Praise him, sun and moon;
    Praise him, all you shining stars!

4   Praise him, you highest heavens,
    and you waters above the heavens!

5   Let them praise the name of the Lord,
    for he commanded and they were created.

6   He established them for ever and ever;
    he fixed their bounds, which cannot be passed.

7   Praise the Lord from the earth,
    you sea monsters and all deeps,

8   fire and hail, snow and frost,
    stormy wind fulfilling his command!

9   Mountains and all hills,
    fruit trees and all cedars!

10 Wild animals and all cattle,
    creeping things and flying birds!

11 Kings of the earth and all people,
    princes and all rulers of the earth!

12 Young men and women alike,
    old and young together!

13 Let them praise the name of the LORD,
    for his name alone is exalted;
    his glory is above earth and heaven.

14 He has raised up a horn for his people,
praise for all his faithful,
for the people of Israel who are close to him.
Praise the LORD!

a. *Introduction*

Ps. 148 is third in the group of five Hallelujah psalms that conclude the book (146-150). This psalm summons all in the heavens and all on earth to praise Yahweh. Human beings, particularly the Jews, join in this praise.[146] It is a late communal hymn of praise to the Creator. Its literary antecedents are from a tradition of hymnody common to Israel and Mesopotamia (Isa. 44:23, Ps. 103:20-22).[147] The whole universe, the creation, is called upon, in this psalm, to join in the choir that praises the name of Yahweh. The effect of Ps. 148 is to articulate God's universal sovereignty. This poem was certainly inspired and copied in the "Song of the Three Young Men" (*benedicite*) from the burning fiery furnace (see Daniel 3:52-90).[148] The call to praise proceeds rather from the wish that all creatures may participate in the joy at the glory which Yahweh has bestowed upon his people after their deep humiliation.[149]

"Praise the Lord" is what begins and ends Ps. 148. It displays the typical structure of a song of praise: invitation to praise, followed by reasons for praise. Here the invitation is greatly elaborated. The word "praise" (*hallel*) occurs eleven times as a verb and once as a noun (v. 14). The intent to be universal is reinforced by the prepositional phrases in vv. 1, 7 and by the repetition

---

[146] Briggs and Briggs, *The Book of Psalms*, 538.

[147] Brown et al., eds., *The New Jerome Biblical Commentary*, 551.

[148] See Weiser, *The Psalms*, 837.

[149] See Delitzsch, *Psalms*, 405.

of "all" in vv. 2-3, 7, 9-11, 14. In this psalm, there is everyone and everything that praises God.[150] This hymn is an expression of the praiseworthiness of Yahweh. The psalmist calls upon all creatures in heaven and on earth, and more specially humankind of all types and classes and races and ages, to join in concert in praise of the name of Yahweh.[151]

b. Structure

As Weiser describes it, the psalm has an architectural structure, "starting with the heaven (vv. 1-6), the call to praise God descends to the earth (vv. 7-10), then turns to mankind (vv. 11-13) and ends (vv. 13-14) with the community of God's people, in whose midst the divine salvation which is the cause and the theme of the hymn became visible and actual."[152] For practical purpose, we shall look at the structure as follows:

> 148:1-6: Praise from the heaven
> 7-14: Praise from the earth.

This psalm can still be divided as follows:

> 148:1-2: The summons of celestial beings
> 3-4: The heavens of heavens
> 5-6: The invitation to praise the name
> 7-8: Praise from the earth
> 9-10: Appeal to cattle and reptiles
> 11-12: Summons to all classes of society
> 13-14: Israel, a people close to God.[153]

---

[150] McCann Jr., "The Book of Psalms," 1271.
[151] See Delitzsch, *Psalms,* 404.
[152] Weiser, *The Psalms,* 837.
[153] See Terrien, *The Psalms,* 919-921.

c. Interpretation

The usual pattern of a hymn can graphically be put as follows: "Praise—you—the Lord—because/for he is/has done." Ps. 148 is an elaboration of one member, "you," of the paradigm. It multiplies those invited or called to praise Yahweh.

The Summons of Celestial Beings (vv. 1-2)

The psalm begins and ends with "Praise the Lord" (*hallelujah*). It is disputed whether they are editorial additions or part of the composition itself. In our song, they seem to fit well into the nature and structure of the hymn. God is to be praised "from the heavens" (v. 1) by the beings and objects that inhabit the heavens. All things created by God and maintained by him are called upon to praise him. Celestial elements are personified and become beings, like angels and the heavenly host, sons of God. The poet lyrically associates the whole universe with the hymnic symphony and chorus that he will direct in the course of a service of thanksgiving.[154]

The Heavens of Heavens (vv. 3-4)

The psalmist exhorts the moon, the sun, and the stars to join the concert and to render praise truly universal. He wishes to invite the totality of creation by summoning the heavens par excellence.[155]

The Invitation to Praise the Name (vv. 5-6)

The poet now unveils the secret purpose of the hymn: "Let them praise the name of the Lord" (v. 5). Creation is the subtone of

---

[154] Ibid., 919.
[155] Ibid., 920.

"the name." YHWH means "He who causes to be" and not "I am" of the LXX.[156] The translation of v. 6b has been subjected to discussion. It may be rendered in three ways: "He set a law 1) and he will not be transgressed; 2) and they will not transgress it (or it will not be transgressed); and 3) it will not change." The last two are the ones usually favoured by the scholars. NRSV has chosen "he fixed their bounds, which cannot be passed." Whichever is chosen, the general meaning is clear, and it appears to be the following: a fixed bound is set to the nature and activity of each in its mutual relation to all, and no one transgresses this law given to it.

"In heaven (vv. 1-6) there are the astral singers: angels, sun, moon, shining stars, heavenly spaces, and the waters above the heavens, that is, the rains."[157] The parts of the psalm are based on the theme "heavens and earth." The first part concerns the praise of the Lord "from the heavens" (v. 1) and the second "from the earth" (v. 7).[158]

Praise from the Earth (vv. 7-8)

All the inhabitants of the land and sea are also invited to join the celestial choir in praising the Lord. The "sea monsters," "fire and hail," and "snow and frost" (more correctly "smoke," one of the elements in a theophany) are the first ones called upon to laud Yahweh. Here the stress is on the fact that they perform God's word and in their grandeur and their relatedness to the whole of creation that is destined to glorify God. Hence their destructive powers are not at all referred to. The wind is portrayed as fulfilling God's order (v. 8). It is God's messenger or servant sent out by him at the moment of creation and at decisive moments in the history

---

[156]   Ibid., 920.
[157]   Farmer, *International Bible Commentary*, 915.
[158]   Mays, *Psalms*, 444.

of salvation. In the beginning, "a wind from God swept over the face of the waters" (Gen. 1:2). During the exodus, "The Lord drove the sea back by a strong east wind all night, and turned the sea into dry land; and the waters were divided" (Ex. 14:21).

Appeal to Cattle and Reptiles (vv. 9-10)

"Mountains and all hills" (v. 9) is a stereotyped couple, and the expression implies that even all that is elevated submit to God and praise him. This is true also of "cattle" (v. 10), which refers to tame animals. "Wild animals" and "cattle" are polar expressions and point to the totality. This is also true of the "creeping things" (reptiles) and "flying birds" (v. 10). The whole of the animal kingdom glorifies God. Here there is an example of merism: wild animals and cattle.

Summons to All Classes of Society (vv. 11-12)

The culminating focus in Ps. 148 is on humanity (vv. 11-12). In v. 12, the psalmist probably eyes the religious community gathered in Jerusalem for worship (cf. Joel 2:16-17). The old religious community (Israel) has been wonderfully restored (cf. Ezra 3:1, 6:21), and they can celebrate their nearness to him, set apart as they are to engage in his service and to enjoy his blessing (cf. Ex. 19:6, Lev. 10:3, Ps. 65:4, Isa. 61:6).[159] All people, irrespective of their status, age, or sex, are called upon to render praise.[160] Here there is a listing of all peoples of the earth, kings, princes, and judges, down to the youth, even to young girls and old people. The social status does not matter. Even maidens are invited to sing praises in a predominantly male culture, where females were ignored.[161]

---

[159]   See Allen, *Psalms 101-150,* 317.
[160]   See Anderson, *Psalms,* Vol. 2, 951.
[161]   See Terrien, *The Psalms,* 921.

Israel, a People Close to God (vv. 13-14)

Earth and heaven are syntactically married. Yahweh, "He who causes to be," demands that the realm of God and the realm of humankind be sealed together (Gen. 2:4). In v. 13, you find another merism: earth and heaven. "He has raised up a horn for his people" (v. 14) asserts a reinstatement of the whole people, "all his faithful." The Davidic theology was transferred in the post-exilic era to the whole people. Because God rules the cosmos, God's praise is incomplete without the participation of every voice, human and nonhuman, in heaven and on earth and in all creation.[162] In the psalms, "to raise/exalt the horns" means "to be successful or victorious," and the contrary expression, "to cut off one's horn," signifies "to defeat" (Ps. 75:10). In our context, it stands for to protect or strengthen or dignify.[163]

"On the earth (vv. 7-14) there are twenty-three sinners . . . Monsters, deeps, fire, hail, snow, frost, wind, mountains, hills, fruit trees, cedars, wild beasts, domestic animals, reptiles, birds, kings, peoples, princes, rulers, young men, young women, old people, and children are summoned to praise the Lord."[164]

d. Christian Transposition

1. The angels, divine beings, come to the service of humans. Here there is the unexpected theology of the incarnation.
2. The psalm belongs to the genre of "canticles of creatures" that will have an impressive parallel in Francis of Assisi's

---

162 See McCann Jr., "The Book of Psalms," 1272.
163 See Mays, *Psalms*, 445.
164 See Farmer, *International Bible Commentary*, 915; Weiser, *The Psalms*, 838.

"Canticle of Brother Sun," in which he addresses the sun and wind and fire as brother, and the moon and water and earth as sister. On the basis of Ps. 148, we can speak of a "symbiosis in praise" involving humans and nature. Human beings are called to exercise their God-given "dominion" or sovereignty in the same way that God exercises power: as a servant. To so fulfill our vocation is to praise God by imitating him.[165]

3. This psalm implies and demonstrates the inseparability of theology and ecology.

4. Ps. 148 is a psalm for Christmas and for Easter and for all seasons. The Christmas hymn, "Joy to the World," is a paraphrase of Ps. 148, another hymn that proclaims God's reign and invites universal recognition in praise.

---

[165] See McCann Jr., "The Book of Psalms," 1272.

II. PSALMS OF DECLARATIVE PRAISE (THANKSGIVING PSALMS)

With Hermann Gunkel, we can say that the songs of thanks shout for joy over the specific deed that God has just performed for the one giving thanks.[166] In Westermann's language, a thanksgiving psalm is "declarative praise." They are of two types: personal/private or national/communal. They can be also called declarative praises of the individual or the people.

Before we look at this genre more closely, here are a few remarks:

1) Form critics are not unanimous about this classification.
2) Thanksgiving psalms are related, on the one hand, to hymns or psalms of praise and, on the other, to laments.

A. Psalms of Declarative Praise (Thanksgiving Psalms) of the Individual

The word "thanksgiving" comes from the Hebrew *todah,* which can denote a song of thanksgiving as well as a thanksgiving sacrifice.[167] A divine intervention in a situation of suffering is celebrated or remembered in a thanksgiving psalm of the individual. Its typical elements include:

- Expressions of praise and gratitude to God
- Description of the trouble or distress from which the psalmist has been delivered
- Testimony of others concerning God's saving deeds

---

[166] Gunkel and Begrich, *Einleitung in die Psalmen,* 276.
[167] H. H. Guthrie, *Israel's Sacred Songs,* New York, 1978, 149.

- Exhortation to others to join praising God and acknowledging God's ways[168]

a. Its Setting in Life

The liturgical thanksgiving ceremony is the setting against which we have to look for the thanksgiving psalms of the individual. The one delivered from an affliction is to be seen as coming to the temple, full of joy, accompanied by family and friends, on occasions, even carrying a sacrificial animal. The vow made by the individual is thus fulfilled, culminating, at times, in a sacrifice of thanksgiving with the accompanying meal. Ps. 118 seems to include all the elements of a typical liturgy of thanksgiving.

b. Structure of an Individual Thanksgiving Psalm

The following are some of the structural elements of a personal thanksgiving song:

1) An introduction in the form of a call to sing, give thanks, and so on (Ps. 9:1-2, 30:1, 107:1).
2) The body of the psalm contains some of the elements given below:

   i) An account of trouble and salvation (narrative). It can be expressed in a formula: "In my affliction I cried to Yahweh and he heard me." This is one of the more important elements of thanksgiving. Invariably, it includes a description of the trouble in which one found oneself.

---

168   McCann Jr., "The Book of Psalms," 647.

This person seeks help from God, who answers through an intervention (Ps. 30:2-3, 40:2-3, 138:3).

ii) Confession of Yahweh as saviour from distress. The Hebrew word *todah* also contains the nuance of "confess to." Thanks thus becomes a proclamation of the faithfulness of God before humans (Ps. 18:1-3, 40:5, 118:28).

iii) Announcement of a sacrifice. It may or may not be present in this type of songs (Ps. 66:13-15, 116:17-18).

iv) Blessings upon participants (Ps. 30:11-12).

3) A conclusion is found in some of these psalms (Ps. 30:11-12).

9:1-2: Declaration of gratitude

3-6: Narrative

7-12: Description of God's justice to the bystanders

13-18: Narrative

19-20: Conclusion

32:1-2: Declaration

3-5: Narrative

6-11: Confession and exhortation to bystanders

i. Ps. 30: Thanksgiving for Recovery from Grave Illness

1 I will extol you, O LORD, for you have drawn me up,
and did not let my foes rejoice over me.

2 O LORD my God, I cried to you for help,
and you have healed me.

3 O LORD, you brought up my soul from Sheol,
restored me to life from among those gone down to the Pit.

4 Sing praises to the LORD, O you his faithful ones,
and give thanks to his holy name.

5   For his anger is but for a moment;
     his favour is for a lifetime.
     Weeping may linger for the night,
     but joy comes with the morning.

6   As for me, I said in my prosperity,
     "I shall never be moved."

7   By your favour, O LORD,
     you had established me as a strong mountain;
     you hid your face;
     I was dismayed.

8   To you, O LORD, I cried
     and to the LORD I made supplication:

9   "What profit is there in my death,
     if I go down to the Pit?
     Will the dust praise you?
     will it tell of your faithfulness?

10 Hear, O Lord, and be gracious to me!
     O LORD, be my helper!"

11 You have turned my mourning into dancing;
     you have taken off my sackcloth
     and clothed me with joy,

12 So that my soul may praise you and not be silent.
     O LORD my God, I will give thanks to you forever.

a. Introduction

Psalm 30 is a prayer of thanksgiving (declarative praise of an individual) for deliverance in the form of acknowledgement.[169] The introduction of the psalm is "A song at the dedication of the temple." The annual feast of the dedication (*Hanukkah*) commemorates the purification of the temple from pagan worship at the time of Judas Maccabaeus. It took place c. 164/165 BC (1 Macc. 4:42-60). It was also celebrated in memory of the miraculous deliverance of the people from the Syrian overlordship (1 Macc. 4:52ff., 2 Macc. 10:1ff., Jn 10:22). The psalm may have been used earlier in connection with the dedication of the second temple in the sixth century (Ezra 4:16-18, Neh. 12:27-43). After 165 BC, the life setting of the psalm was *Hanukkah*.[170] Exegetes are agreed that it is a later addition, since the psalm is likely to be much older than second century BC.[171] Originally it was a thanksgiving of an individual who had been restored from a serious illness. What we have in the introduction, then, is the reinterpretation of the experiences of an individual as referring to those of the community.[172]

The composer composed a pattern of alteration and reversal through the entire poem: "I cried—you healed me" (v. 2); "anger—favour" (v. 5a); "divine favour—hid your face" (v. 7); "weeping—joy (v. 5b); "mourning—dancing" (v. 11). Ps. 30 has some verbal connections with the prayer of King Hezekiah when he was sick (Isa. 38) and with Ps. 6. Recovery from serious illness

---

169 Mays, *Psalms,* 139; Craigie, *Psalms 1-50,* 251; Brown et al., eds., *The New Jerome Biblical Commentary,* 531.

170 See Mays, *Psalms,* 140; Anderson, *Psalms,* 239.

171 See McCann Jr., "The Book of Psalms," 795.

172 See Anderson, *Psalms,* 239.

is the deliverance reported in v. 2.[173] In this psalm, the importance of the praise of God is the basis (v. 9) and the goal of prayer (v. 12).

b. Structure

> 30:1-3: Thanks to God for the deliverance
> 4-5: Call to the congregation to praise Yahweh
> 6-10: Description of his past experiences
> 11-12: Celebration of return to health.

c. Interpretation

30:1-3: Thanks to God for the deliverance

This passage is dominated by four verbs of action credited to Yahweh:

> You have *drawn* me up (v. 1).
> You have *healed* me (v. 2b).
> You have *brought up* my soul (v. 3a).
> You have *restored* me to life (v. 3b).

"I will extol you, O Lord" (v. 1) identifies the purpose of the song. To extol or exalt Yahweh means to recognise him as the Exalted One in all his graciousness (cf. Isa. 25:1). To extol and to thank go together. Any sick person was judged by enemies as one abandoned by Yahweh. The patient happily recognised that his plague was only a temporary ailment. Yahweh was praised because he has drawn him up (v. 1). The picture painted by the author reveals to us that just as a bucket is drawn up from a well or a prisoner lifted up from a dungeon, so God has snatched

---

[173] See Mays, *Psalms*, 139-140.

him away from the peril of death. The foes are the people who jeer at his faith. Their triumph would naturally have meant their triumph over his faith as well. In time of medical crisis, he has prayed for help, and God has answered his prayer (v. 2).

Sheol (3) is a frequently occurring term in the psalms. Other words like "pit" (28:1), "death" (6:5), "earth" (71:20), and "abandon" (88:11) are used as synonyms of *sheol*. It is the realm of the dead (49:11), the counterpart to the Greek (English) "Hades." It was a land of no return (Job 7:9), the abode of all: rich or poor, Israelite or foreigner. It was characterised by silence (94:17), darkness (143:3), weakness, and helplessness (88:4-6). Its occupants were cut off from the land of the living and also from fellowship with God (88:5). In the OT, in general, the abode of the dead is not regarded as a place of punishment or torment. The idea of hell is a product of the Hellenistic period. In our song, his statement about *sheol* and the "pit" indicates how grievous his suffering had been and how profound his abandonment by God was.

30:4-5: Call to the Congregation to Praise Yahweh

In harmony with the nature of the OT covenant, the personal experience of God gained by one individual is not exclusively his own but also the concern of the cult community. The poet finds it possible to express (v. 5) as a universal truth what has first come to him as an entirely personal experience. God's anger is for a moment, but his favour is for a lifetime. This has been the experience of the afflicted one. In other words, "the purpose of God's anger is not to destroy but to educate."[174] A thought (cf. v. 5cd) is very picturesquely put by Delitzsch: "In the evening weeping takes its abode with us

---

[174]   Weiser, *The Psalms*, 270.

for the night, but in the morning another guest, viz. joy appears, like a rescuing angel, before whom weeping disappears."[175]

30:6-10: Description of His Past Experience

Verse 6 describes the worshipper's past attitude of arrogant self-confidence: "I shall never be moved" (v. 6). He had blissfully forgotten that his life was wholly dependent on God. This truth became stunningly clear to him when the Lord hid his face from him (v. 7), that is, when sickness pinned him to his bed and imminent death threatened him. The above fact gave him a realisation of his sin, and thus he fell on his knees in prayer (v. 8). In his petition, he enquires, "Will the dust praise you?" (v. 9). "Dust" can mean here either the grave or those who dwell in the dust (i.e., the dwellers in the underworld). The idea of "praise" is connected with the sad fact of the lack of communion between those in hell and Yahweh.[176] "Praise has a theological basis as well as an anthropological one. Praise is the way the faithfulness of the Lord becomes word and is heard in the Lord's world (v. 9). For people, it is the language of joy and gladness that goes with life and is life in contrast to the silence of death" (vv. 11-12).[177]

30:11-12: Celebration of Return to Health

The prayer of the sufferer has been heard. Yahweh has come to his help. As a result, he is clothed with gladness. "Sackcloth" (v. 11) is the symbol of penitence or mourning. Because of the transformation brought about in his life, he will thank God forever (v. 12): as long as he lives.[178]

---

[175] Delitzsch, *Psalms,* 377.
[176] See Weiser, *The Psalms,* 270-172.
[177] Mays, *Psalms,* 141.
[178] See Weiser, *The Psalms,* 272.

Looking at the psalm as a whole, we find in it the presence of a series of polarities: anger and favour, weeping and joy, night and morning (5); mourning and dancing (11); and so on. "In this series of opposites," says Luis Alonso Schokel, "we recognise ourselves. Human existence is not only subject to them, it realises itself in them."[179] These extremes seem to delimit the frontiers of our experience. Underlying the above pairs, there is one that governs all the others: death and life. "Weeping," "mourning," and "night" can stand for death, and "joy," "mourning," and "dancing" can symbolise life. The author has experienced a sort of going down to death and then, through God's intervention, the rising to life.

d. Christian Transposition

Jesus, as man, experienced this polarity in his own life. Not only that, he descended to the abyss of death. But God's power reached down into his tomb to raise him up. Restored to life, he is about to sing God's praises and thank him forever. Christ, thus, exhausts this polarity in his own person.[180]

Death need not be only the demise of the body, but also the disruption of the covenant relationship with God.[181]

Suffering need not be an indication of the absence of God for those who take refuge in God (Ps. 2:12). The existence of suffering does not negate the good news that life is a gift from God.[182]

---

[179] L. Alonso Schokel, "Psalm 30 as Christian Prayer," *Homiletic and Pastoral Review* 72(10), 1972: 23.

[180] Ibid., 22-27.

[181] Craigie, *Psalms 1-50*, 255.

[182] See McCann Jr., "The Book of Psalms," 797.

Ps. 30 is appropriate for Easter, because it is an affirmation of both God's life-giving power and life as God's good gift. The psalmist's deliverance is not so much from physical sickness to physical health as it is from a deadly misunderstanding of human security (vv. 6-7) to a lively awareness of God's presence in all of life (vv. 11-12).[183]

ii. Ps. 118: A Liturgy of Thanksgiving

1   O give thanks to the LORD, for he is good;
    his steadfast love endures forever!

2   Let Israel say,
    "His steadfast love endures forever."

3   Let the house of Aaron say,
    "His steadfast love endures forever."

4   Let those who fear the LORD say,
    "His steadfast love endures forever."

5   Out of my distress I called on the LORD;
    the LORD answered me and set me in a broad place.

6   With the LORD on my side I do not fear.
    What can mortals do to me?

7   The LORD is on my side to help me;
    I shall look in triumph on those who hate me.

8   It is better to take refuge in the LORD
    than to put confidence in mortals.

---

[183]   Ibid., 797.

9 It is better to take refuge in the LORD
   than to put confidence in princes.

10 All nations surrounded me;
    in the name of the LORD I cut them off!

11 They surrounded me, surrounded me on every side;
    in the name of the LORD I cut them off!

12 They surrounded me like bees;
    they blazed like a fire of thorns;
    in the name of the LORD I cut them off!

13 I was pushed hard, so that I was falling;
    but the LORD helped me.

14 The LORD is my strength and my might;
    he has become my salvation.

15 There are glad songs of victory in the tents of the righteous:
    "The right hand of the LORD does valiantly;

16 the right hand of the LORD is exalted;
    the right hand of the LORD does valiantly."

17 I shall not die, but I shall live,
    and recount the deeds of the LORD.

18 The LORD has punished me severely,
    but he did not give me over to death.

19 Open to me the gates of righteousness,
    that I may enter through them
    and give thanks to the LORD.

20 This is the gate of the LORD;
   the righteous shall enter through it.

21 I thank you that you have answered me
   and have become my salvation.

22 The stone that the builders rejected
   has become the chief cornerstone.

23 This is the LORD's doing;
   it is marvelous in our eyes.

24 This is the day that the LORD has made;
   let us rejoice and be glad in it.

25 Save us, we beseech you, O LORD!
   O LORD, we beseech you, give us success!

26 Blessed is the one who comes in the name of LORD.
   We bless you from the house of the LORD.

27 The LORD is God,
   and he has given us light
   Bind the festal procession with branches
   up to the horns of the altar.

28 You are my God, and I will give thanks to you;
   you are my God, I will extol you.

29 O give thanks to the LORD, for he is good,
   for his steadfast love endures forever.

a. Introduction

Martin Luther viewed Ps. 118 as "my own beloved psalm."[184] It appears to have been composed by a skillful organiser. It is ordinarily categorised as a liturgy of thanksgiving, because it provides a paradigm of the cultic action with which such a song was accompanied.[185] In this liturgy, the king, the priests, the Levites, and the people share various parts. The dialogue is so real that the scene is almost re-enacted before our very eyes. The speaker in the psalm reveals himself both in the first person singular and the third person plural. Hence there is a discussion among scholars whether Ps. 118 is to be viewed as individual, communal, or both.[186]

A difficult, unique, and impressive Ps. 118 is the last of the "Egyptian (Passover) Hallel" (113-118), which was recited every year on Passover night in remembrance of the exodus. Both exodus and deliverance from exile served as a basis for hope that future deliverance would also occur.[187] "'The Lord is my strength' (v. 14) stands out between the beginning and the ending of the psalm, with the declaration, 'The Lord is good' (vv. 1 and 29)."[188] Psalm 118 stands in favour of a pre-exilic or post-exilic date.

b. Structure

118:1-4: Congregational thanksgiving
5-18: First hymn of thanksgiving

---

184 McCann Jr., "The Book of Psalms," 1156.
185 See Stuhlmuller, *Psalms*, 147-148; Allen, *Psalms 101-150*, 122, 124; Mays, *Psalms*, 375.
186 See McCann Jr., "The Book of Psalms," 1153.
187 Ibid., 1153; Anderson, *Psalms*, 779-780; Mays, *Psalms*, 378.
188 Terrien, *The Psalms*, 781.

19-28: Second hymn of thanksgiving
29: Conclusion

c. Interpretation

118:1-4: Congregational Thanksgiving

The opening and concluding invitations (vv. 1-4, 29) provide a framework for the recital of vv. 5-18 outside the temple gate and celebration of deliverance in vv. 19-28, inside the temple court.[189] The psalm is introduced and concluded by the liturgical formula "O give thanks to the Lord, for he is good; his steadfast love endures forever."

His "steadfast love" that describes the very essence of God's character features the invitations. Verses 2-4 anticipate the communal dimension, a hymnic thanksgiving of the people. The Levites, probably, initiate the invitation to give thanks to the Lord, and the assembly responds to it. Those called upon to do this are "Israel," the people of the covenant at large; the "house of Aaron," the priestly caste; and "those who fear the Lord," the proselytes of non-Israelite origin who have been invited to be present at this special service,[190] or the more faithful Jews. Fear of the Lord is the essential disposition of every believer who adores Yahweh. The above groups are invited to proclaim his "steadfast love" (*hesed*) which, applied to God, implies his total loyalty in love to the covenant partner.

118:5-18: First Hymn of Thanksgiving

118:5-18 can be divided into vv. 5-9 (the psalmist's trust in Yahweh); vv. 10-14 (the battle with the nations); and vv. 15-18

---

189   See Mays, *Psalms*, 374.
190   See Weiser, *The Psalms*, 725; Knight, *Psalms*, 206.

(victory shout). This hymn is sung in the city of Jerusalem, where the procession begins. "In distrust we must have a lively trust in the God who leads us to complete and triumphant victory."[191] The main actor in this section is an individual—in all likelihood the king, whose thanksgiving follows. In vv. 5-7, he begins the narrative by referring, in general terms, to the prior distress in which he found himself. Verses 8-9 are a comment, in wisdom style, on vv. 6-7 made by the priests. "There is only *one* place where we can take our stand without ever being shaken and that is at God's side."[192]

The king picks up the thread of the narrative in 10-12 and describes his danger vividly. The fourfold repetition of "surrounded me" pictures him as cut off from all sides. Nay more, he was encircled, as by bees. Verse 12b is amenable to two translations: "they blazed like a fire of thorns." The line would then point to the fierceness of the attack. The other alternative is "they were extinguished like a fire of thorns," implying thereby that the hostilities were checked in no time. He is immediately saved by God. He fights in the name of Yahweh and wards off his enemies. Finally, in deep humility, he acknowledges him in whose name the victory was gained.

Verse 15ab may be a later addition. "The tents of the righteous" could indicate the tents of the pilgrims. But the word used here is *ohel*, not the one usually employed at that time for a pilgrim's tent. Secondly, it could refer to the temple, but the normal expression for that would be the "tent of Yahweh." Thirdly, it could stand for the houses of Jerusalem, and this appears to be the more probable meaning here.

---

[191] Gianfranco Ravasi, "Psalms 90-150," in *The International Bible Commentary*, edited by William R. Farmer (Bangalore: TPI, 2004), 907.

[192] Weiser, *The Psalms*, 726.

118:19-28: Second Hymn of Thanksgiving

It seems that some sort of liturgical procession originally lay behind vv. 19-28. There is a dialogue between priests and faithful (vv. 19-20). There is the acclamation addressed to the unyielding "stone" of the temple, which symbolises Yahweh, the rock of safety (vv. 21-25). There is the priestly blessing (vv. 26-27) and the response of the king (v. 28). We do not exactly know the significance of the expression "the gates of righteousness." It could be the symbolic name of one of the gates of the temple, as, for example, was the custom in Babylon, or the door through which the righteous were to enter the holy place or the gate of the just God and so on.

Once inside the temple, the king advances toward the altar, proclaiming once again the marvel that God worked in his life: "The stone that the builders rejected has become the chief cornerstone" (v. 22).[193] It is a proverbial saying applied to this context in order to bring out the radical reversal of fortunes, of deliverance from death to life. God brings about a radical change in his life, that is tantamount to an inversion of human plans and projects. It would have served in the post-exilic era to interpret the experience of the people as well (see Isa. 28:16, Jer. 51:26).[194] The stone which is the "chief cornerstone" alludes either to one of the large cornerstones that binds together two rows of stones or to the keystone (copestone) that completes an arch or structure. A stone considered unimportant has now become prominent.

The shift to the plural in the psalm is clear in vv. 23-27. The reversal of fortunes is unambiguously attributed to God, and the vocabulary of vv. 23-24 continues to recall the exodus

---

193   See Allen, *Psalms 101-150*, 125.
194   See McCann Jr., "The Book of Psalms," 1155.

as a prototype. The shift in v. 25 to "save us, we beseech you" is a real and urgent petition. After receiving the blessing from Yahweh, the people affirm their faith in Yahweh as God.[195] The petition in v. 25 orients the psalm to the future as well as to the past and thus gives the psalm an open-endedness that is evident in the history of its use. "Save us" (v. 25) comes from Hebrew *hosi'ahana,* transliterated as "hosanna," the shorter form. In the OT, it is used as a cry for help, but in the NT it is a greeting or acclamation.[196] "Bind the festal procession with branches up to the horns of the altar" (27bc) is a mysterious verse, as the Hebrew text is not clear. It refers to a rite initiated, probably, at the order of the Levites. It could signify some sort of festal procession or dance, possibly around the altar, which, in later times, included the waving of branches. "The horns of the altar" were projections at its four corners. They were counted as the most important or sacred parts of the altar. At one time, to hold onto the horns of the altar was equivalent to a claim for divine protection (1 Kgs 2:28).[197]

The psalmist reaffirms the intent to give thanks (see vv. 1, 19,21) and invites the community to participate (v. 29).

d. Christian Transposition

Ps. 118 occupies an important place in New Testament theology.

"The early Christian community identified the speaker in vv. 5-18, 28 as Jesus . . . . When Jesus entered Jerusalem shortly before his crucifixion, he was greeted by a crowd in a manner reminiscent of Ps. 118. In Mk 11:9, the first part of the greeting

---

[195] See Allen, *Psalms 101-150,* 125.

[196] See Anderson, *Psalms, 803.*

[197] Anderson, *Psalms,* 805; see Knight, *Psalms,* 212.

consists of Ps. 118:25a, 26a . . . . Verses 22-23 were understood within first century Judaism to refer to the Messiah. In fact, Mt. 21:42 cites these verses to suggest that Jesus is the rejected Messiah (see also Luke 20:17 ; Acts 4:11-12). In the story of Jesus' entry into Jerusalem, the Gospel writers have extended the messianic interpretation to vv. 25-26 . . . . For all the Gospel writers, Psalm 118 is a means of understanding and articulating the significance of Jesus."[198]

"All four evangelists use it in the Palm Sunday narrative (Matt 19:9; Mark 11:9-10; Luke 19:38; John 12:13), generally associating it with Zech. 9:9. 'Hosanna,' the equivalent of 'save' in 118:25, became used as a joyful shout of acclamation. According to Mark 12:10-11 (cf. 8:31; Matt 23:29; Luke 13:35), Jesus applied vv. 22-23 to his coming passion and resurrection, and they ring out again on Peter's lips in Acts 4:11. V. 22 of the psalm became an important element in the theological stone imagery of Eph. 2:20-21 and 1 Pet. 2:4-8. Underlying the citation of v. 6 in Heb. 3:6 is doubtless a sense of the Christian community's oneness with the glorified Christ."[199]

As José Luis Sicre affirms, "Early Christianity saw in the marvelous work of God depicted in the psalms the destiny of Jesus . . . . He is 'the one exalted by the right hand of God' (v. 16), the 'cornerstone' (v. 22), 'he who comes' (v. 26). And the psalm continues open, awaiting future fulfillment, because Christ must return."[200]

---

[198]   McCann Jr., "The Book of Psalms," 1156.
[199]   Allen, *Psalms 101-150*, 125. See Mays, *Psalms*, 379-380; Delitzsch, *Psalms*, 229-230.
[200]   José Luis Sicre, "Psalm 118 and New Testament Christology," *TD* 26 (1978): 144.

"Psalm 118 has become in Christian liturgical tradition not just a psalm for Palm/Passion Sunday, which celebrates Jesus' entry into Jerusalem, but also for Easter Sunday. For Christians, Easter is above all 'the day on which the Lord has acted' (v. 24, NEB). God was active in the exodus; God was active in returning exiles; God was active in the life, death, and resurrection of Jesus. So the Gospel writers affirm in their use of Psalm 118."[201]

iii. Ps. 138: Thanksgiving and Praise

1. I give you thanks, O LORD, with my whole heart;
   before the gods I sing your praise;

2. I bow down toward your holy temple
   and give thanks to your name for your steadfast love and
   your faithfulness.
   For you have exalted your name and your word
   above everything.

3. On the day I called, you answered me,
   you increased my strength of soul.

4. All the kings of the earth shall praise you, O LORD,
   for they have heard the words of your mouth.

5. They shall sing of the ways of the LORD,
   for great is the glory of the LORD.

6. For though the LORD is high, he regards the lowly;
   but the haughty he perceives from far away.

---

[201] McCann Jr., "The Book of Psalms," 1156; see Mays, *Psalms,* 380-381.

7. Though I walk in the midst of trouble,
   you preserve me against the wrath of my enemies;
   you stretch out your hand,
   and your right hand delivers me.

8. The LORD will fulfill his purpose for me;
   your steadfast love, O LORD, endures forever.
   Do not forsake the work of your hands.

a. Introduction

Ps. 138, a declarative praise psalm (thanksgiving song), is an individual human being's response to God's gracious intervention.[202] According to Dahood, it is a royal song of thanksgiving.[203] Here the worshipper addresses God directly, not speaking *about* God but referring to the great works of God in general. A unique feature of Ps. 138 is that it recalls Ps. 135:5 and 136:2-3 ("Our Lord is above all gods"). Ps. 138:2, 3, 5, 8 bring out God's "name" (see Ps. 135:1, 3), proclaim God's greatness (see 135:5), and invite people to be grateful to God's "steadfast love" (136:1-3, 26). We can, therefore, say with Mays that Psalm 138 "can be understood as a general song of praise by the restored community in the post-exilic period, written under the influence of the prophets whose words are gathered in Isaiah 40-66."[204]

---

[202] See McCann Jr., "The Book of Psalms," 1231; Kselman and Barré, *Psalms,* 550; Terrien, *The Psalms,* 869; Mays, *Psalms,* 424; Allen, *Psalms 101-150,* 245.

[203] See Mitchell Dahood, *Psalms III,* 101-150. W. F. Albright and D. N. Friedman, eds., The Anchor Bible (New York: Doubleday, 1970), 276.

[204] McCann Jr. "The Book of Psalms," 1231.

The more likely date for the composition of the psalm is post-exilic.[205] According to Dahood, Ps. 138 comes from the Davidic period.

b. Structure

Structurally, the declarative praise psalms consist of three main parts: introduction, main section, and conclusion. The introduction consists of an invocation of Yahweh and the declaration of intent. The main section involves an account of the distress experienced and of God's deliverance. The conclusion includes an invitation to praise or thank Yahweh.[206]

> 138:1-3: Thanksgiving for deliverance
> 4-6: Universal homage to Yahweh
> 7-8: Confidence in Yahweh's covenant loyalty

c. Interpretation

Psalm 138:1-3: The Thanksgiving for Deliverance

Ps. 138 is a thanksgiving to Yahweh for his kindness and faithfulness (vv. 1-3). The psalmist "praises" Yahweh and "gives thanks" to him "with my whole heart" (v. 1). This attitude of his indicates that his intellect and his will are not divided, a rejection of tensions between faith and doubt. "Gods" (*elohim*) (v. 1) may mean "heavenly beings." The Israelite king proclaims his faith in Yahweh. "I bow down toward your holy temple" (v. 2a) is to profess that God alone is sovereign, the sole provider for one's life. God manifests to him "steadfast love" and "faithfulness" (v.

---

[205]   See Ravasi, *Psalms 90-150,* 912; Mays, *Psalms,* 424.
[206]   See Anderson, *Psalms,* Vol. 1, 35-36.

2b). They constitute God's self-manifestation made to Moses (Ex. 34:6-7) and became part of a basic profession of Israel's faith. Thus they become the basis for an appeal to God for help and as a profession of trust. Having experienced God's "steadfast love," one can assume a new power to love others. V. 2c emphasises God's dependability and suggests that the Israelite king finds himself abroad, where heathen deities are worshipped. He was probably on a military expedition.

Psalm 138:4-6: Universal Homage to Yahweh

Athenasius called this song "the psalm of the universal call to salvation."[207] "All the kings of the earth shall praise you, O LORD" (v. 4) implies that the whole world will join in the psalmist's thanksgiving and praise Yahweh (Ps. 68:32, 98:4, 100:1). This implies an interesting touch of universalism.[208] The psalmist's experience is universal, a newly discovered joy of a time when foreign monarchs will praise Yahweh.[209] "The words of your mouth" (v. 4) refers to the promises of Yahweh to the people. Verse 5a asserts that the kings of the earth yield their sovereignty in recognition of God's sovereignty. They celebrate "the ways of the Lord" rather than exercise their own wills. "Ways" (v. 5) may be Yahweh's gracious dealings with Israel. Though "the LORD is high" (v. 6), Yahweh is not too proud to help the least of his creatures (Ps. 113:7-8). "He regards the lowly" (v. 6) means he looks after or looks with favour on the lowest of humankind.[210] In his strength, God has chosen Israel to identify themselves with the underprivileged. He knows the mind of the "haughty," those who despise the others.[211]

---

207   Ravasi, *Psalms 90-150*, 912.
208   See Dahood, *Psalms III*, 278.
209   See Terrien, *The Psalms*, 870.
210   See Terrien, *The Psalms*, 870; Delitzsch, *Psalms*, Vol. 3, 380.
211   See Knight, *Psalms*, 318.

Mathew V. Thekkekara SDB

Psalm 138:7-8: Confidence in Yahweh's Covenant Loyalty

Ps. 138:7-8 portrays the psalmist's personal situation. He affirms that God supports him in his situation of struggle. "You stretch out your hand" (v. 7) describes Yahweh's intervention to help or punish. "Your steadfast love" (v. 8) refers to Yahweh's covenant loyalty. This is the crown of the poem, the final affirmation of praise and a supplication. God has done everything for the psalmist. Yet his world situation is precarious. Hence the final prayer, "Do not forsake the work of your hands."[212]

d. Christian Transposition

"The eschatological perspective of Psalm 138 means that we shall always live in the midst of the fundamental ambiguity that characterises the psalm. That is to say, we shall always find ourselves simultaneously professing God's deliverance (v. 3) and praying for God's deliverance (v. 8c)."[213] This teaches us and calls us to have fundamental dependence upon God. This calls for a dependence, not on ourselves or other gods of our own making, but on God.

Ps. 138:6 recalls Hannah's song (1 Sam. 2:1-10) that is taken up by Mary in anticipation of the birth of Jesus (see Lk. 1:51-53). Jesus distanced himself from the proud and powerful in favour of the lowly. Jesus invites us to live in total dependence upon God and offer one's service to the poor and abandoned.[214]

Ps. 138 is associated with the season of Epiphany, and it invites us to move away from differentiation and distinctions of other persons.

---

[212] See Terrien, *The Psalms*, 870.
[213] McCann Jr. "The Book of Psalms," 1233.
[214] Ibid., 1233.

"The psalm . . . reminds us that salvation comes to us as individuals in community and creates a community that can speak as one in unity. It teaches that our salvation is not first of all and only for our sake but is also and foremost the revelation of the coming kingdom of God. Of that we are to be witnesses to the 'gods' and rulers of the world."[215]

B. Psalms of Declarative Praise (Thanksgiving Psalms) of the Community

These songs follow the same pattern as those of the individual. The only difference between the former and the latter is that God is thanked for his salvific intervention in a communal distress like war, captivity, plague, drought, famine, and so on.

a. Their Setting in Life

Their *Sitz im Leben* is the great festivals of joy held during the recurring pilgrim feasts or the occasion(s) of some special gathering for public thanksgiving after a national catastrophe.

b. Their Structure

Their structural elements are the same as those of the individual psalms.

> 67:1-5: Proper celebrations
> 6: Narrative
> 7: Conclusion

---

[215] Mays, *Psalms,* 425.

124:1-5: Narrative
6-7: Expression of thanksgiving
8: Conclusion

i.   Ps. 65: Thanksgiving for Earth's Bounty

1   Praise is due to you, O God, in Zion;
    and to you shall vows be performed,

2   O you who answer prayer!
    To you all flesh shall come.

3   When deeds of iniquity overwhelm us,
    you forgive our transgressions.

4   Happy are those whom you choose and bring near
    to live in your courts.
    We shall be satisfied with the goodness of your house,
    your holy temple.

5   By awesome deeds you answer us with deliverance,
    O God of our salvation;
    you are the hope of all the ends of the earth
    and of the farthest seas

6   By your strength you established the mountains;
    you are girded with might.

7   You silence the roaring of the seas,
    the roaring of their waves
    the tumult of the peoples.

8   Those who live at earth's farthest bounds are awed by
    your signs;

you make the gate ways of the morning and the evening
shout for joy.

9   You visit the earth and water it,
    you greatly enrich it;
    the river of God is full of water;
    you provide the people with grain,
    for so you have prepared it.

10 You water its furrows abundantly,
    setting its ridges,
    Softening it with showers,
    and blessing its growth.

11 You crown the year with your bounty;
    your wagon tracks overflow with richness.

12 The pastures of the wilderness overflow,
    the hills gird themselves with joy,

13 the meadows clothe themselves with flocks,
    the valleys deck themselves with grain,
    they shout and sing together for joy.

a. Introduction

Ps. 65 is "a National Psalm of thanksgiving which was offered
when a threatening drought and famine had been averted, the
crops were showing a promise of a fine harvest, and the flocks
were greatly increased."[216] That which underlies Ps. 65 is a
prayer for rain requesting God to show the same benevolence
at the beginning of a new agricultural year like his past

---

[216] Anderson, *Psalms,* Vol. 1, 464.

benefits to Israel.[217] It is a national psalm of thanksgiving or a song of praise which was, probably, offered when a threatening drought and famine had been averted through Yahweh's help. The cultic community can be seen as gathered together to fulfill their vow made at the time of distress in a prayer of thanksgiving. "It may be that Psalms 63, 64, and 65 form a concatenation with same thematic continuity."[218]

The song is distinguished from others for its fine poetic sense and language. In it the concrete and the general, the visible and the invisible, the external and the internal, the temporal and the eternal, the things of the past, the present, and the future are being seen and experienced at one and the same time.[219] God is the focal point of the psalmist's thoughts regarding the various things mentioned in the psalm.

b. Structure

"The unity and momentum of this psalm are detected in three key places: v. 2, *you who answer prayer;* v. 5, *you answer us;* and v. 9, *you visit the earth.* From prayer to answer to action!"[220] In vv. 2-4, God hears our prayer; in vv. 5-8, God answers; and in vv. 9-13, God visits the world.

> 65:1-4: God hears prayers
> 5-8: God as creator and redeemer
> 9-13: God as the giver of rain and prosperity

---

[217] Brown et al. *The New Jerome Biblical Commentary,* 536.
[218] Terrien, *The Psalms,* 471.
[219] See Weiser, *The Psalms,* 461.
[220] Stuhlmuller, *Psalms,* 291.

There has been some discussion as to the unity of the psalm. Each of the above three sections possesses a particular style. As a result, some exegetes like Gunkel and Kraus are of the opinion that it is made up of two psalms: vv. 1-8 and 9-13. But difference in style alone is not a sufficiently strong motive for considering it as two psalms. Here we take it to be a single poem.

c. Interpretation

65:1-4: Praise to Zion's God

Approaching God's house evokes in them thoughts about their sinfulness. In the OT, "prayer" (v. 2) is a means of communication between a human being and God. "All flesh" (v. 2) may refer to all human beings; in this case, all of Israel, considered from the point of view of its weaknesses. "Transgressions" (v. 3) are willful sins. Prevalent in Israel was the idea of the casual connection between sin and suffering. That God has removed their distress is evidence of the fact that they have repented of their sins and that God has pardoned them. This forgiving God does "choose and bring near" (v. 4) these persons to dwell in his courts. Such terms are concepts connected with the selection of priests in the OT. In verse 4, they are applied to the people who come to worship. "The goodness of your house" could refer 1) to the delights of the sacrificial banquet; 2) to the nearness of his presence in the sense of the inward spiritual communion with God; and 3) to the hours spent in the temple.

The psalm begins by stating that praise is due to God in Zion. Its theocratic trend is revealed at the outset by the threefold repetition of *le* ("you") in vv. 1-2. The effect is to make God the center of attention from the beginning.[221] "Zion" stands for

---

[221] See Brueggemann, *The Message*, 135.

the Jebusite stronghold that David captured from them (2 Sam. 5:7). It can stand for the temple hill, as in our case, or the city of Jerusalem (Isa. 10:24, 60:14; Ps. 48:2), or Israel (Ps. 149:2, Isa. 46:13), or Judah (Jer. 14:19), or the people of Jerusalem (Ps. 48:11).[222]

65:5-8: God as Creator and Redeemer

As seen in the history of salvation, God listens to the cry of the oppressed and responds with prodigious deeds that bring about their deliverance. People both fear God and are attracted to him. This reality is referred to by the mention of the "awesome deeds" (v. 5) that recalls the exodus (see Ex. 15:11), when God proved to be the "God of our salvation" (v. 5), and after which God's everlasting reign was proclaimed (Ex. 15:18).[223] God's actions of the past are paradigms of his future conduct in favour of all, everywhere and at all times.

Verses 6-7 describe God's work of creation with an emphasis laid on his victory over chaotic and rebellious forces symbolised by the sea. The sea of humanity is also subject to God.

His actions of creation and preservation are recognised by those who live at earth's furthest bounds (v. 8). They are all the inhabitants of the world. The meaning of the word "signs" is not very clear. It could stand for those things through which Yahweh makes known his majesty and power or his deliverance.[224] "The gateways of the morning and the evening" are the east and the

---

[222] See Anderson, *Psalms*, Vol. 1, 465; Marvin E. Tate, *Psalms 51-100. Word Biblical Commentary*, David A. Hubbard et al., eds., Vol. 20 (Dallas: Word Books, 1990), 140.

[223] See McCann Jr., "The Book of Psalms," 934.

[224] See Anderson, *Psalms*, Vol. 1, 470.

west, probably referring to the ends of the earth and those who dwell there. They are made to "shout for joy."

Verses 5-8 can beautifully be summed up in the words of Weiser: "Here . . . belief in God embraces the beginning, the middle, and the end of all earthly happenings and interprets them in the light of their divine purpose as God's dealing with mankind by way of the *Heilsgeschichte* (history of salvation), the aim of which is God's rule over the world; and the festival congregation experience this *Heilsgeschichte* as the present reality of God which they now worship and extol in their hymn."[225]

65:9-13: God as the Giver of Rain and Prosperity

Here there is a sudden change of scene, rhythm, argument, and style. In place of the gigantic visions, the poet focuses his eyes on the near to cull the little. He is not in a hurry to move on; he lingers to take note of every detail that attracts his attention.[226]

The God who performed all the marvels mentioned earlier is pictured here as concentrating on watering the land and making it fertile. The water from the "river of God" (v. 9), that is, the waters above the heavens, softens the hard clods, levels the field, and makes it ready to receive the new seeds. God's tenderness thus becomes concretised in these details. "You water its furrows abundantly" (v. 10) refers to the early rains that softened the ground for ploughing. "Settling its ridges" implies that the rain softened and broke up the clods of earth. "The year" (v. 11) for the Hebrews is not anything abstract but something made alive through God's providential care. "Your wagon tracks overflow with richness" implies an image borrowed from mythology wherein God is pictured as visiting his people on a chariot, and

---

[225] Weiser, *The Psalms,* 465.
[226] See Schokel, *Trenta Salmi,* 285.

wherever the chariot wheels touched the earth, opulence was bestowed on it. In our context, "richness" symbolises the plenty or abundance conferred by God on the land. The marvelous transformation that has come about after the blessing of rain is described in vv. 12-13. In Ps. 65:9-13, there is the praise of God on account of the present year's rich blessing, which he has bestowed upon the land of his people. In vv. 9-10, God is thanked for having sent down the rain required for the ploughing and for the increase of the seed sown, so that, as vv. 11-13 affirm, there is the prospect of a rich harvest.[227] "The barren steppe has been transformed into green pastures; the bare hills are pictured by the poet as living creatures who *'gird themselves with joy'*; the flocks on the green pastures seem to him to be like a festive garment adorning the meadows. The valleys with their rolling cornfields are wrapped in a fresh green garb. Nature awakened to new life is filled with ringing and singing."[228]

As is evident, Ps. 65:9-13 stands among the most descriptive pieces of biblical poetry. It is not, however, a description for its own sake, but one at the service of a theological vision: God is the focal point in all the descriptions. "Psalm 65 is thus another affirmation of the theological heart of the Psalter: God reigns! . . . It is also a reminder to us that we praise God, as also we live, in partnership with heaven and earth and all creation (see esp. vv. 8, 13; see also Psalms 8, 104, 143)."[229]

"The psalm is a succinct masterpiece of theological completeness. It moves from praise to praise . . . . It celebrates a God who is closest to humankind . . . . A God who atones for his children's evil horrors is 'suffering with,' which is the mystery of 'com-passion' and prepares for the Johannine mystery of a God 'who so loved the

---

[227] See Delitzsch, *Psalms*, Vol. 2, 229.
[228] Weiser, *The Psalms*, 466.
[229] McCann, Jr., "The Book of Psalms," 934.

world that he gave his only Son.'"[230] "The strongest impact of the psalm is surely in the joy over the gift of rain and the flourishing growth which results."[231] Ps. 65 insists that thanksgiving is a theological work whose subject is God, not ourselves. It is an antidote to self-satisfaction and self-congratulation.[232]

d. Christian Transposition

1) Ps. 65 reminds us that neither we nor the government rules the world. God rules the world.

2) The liturgy of the dead has borrowed the line: "To thee shall all flesh come on account of sin" (v. 2). The dead are to receive full purification from sin before they can be admitted into the blessedness of the heavenly sanctuary.

3) Zion can be seen as a symbol of the church that is the community of the faithful.

4) It is possible to read the psalm against the background of our Eucharistic liturgy. It has, like the psalm, a penitential part, a section on cosmic and historic praise in the preface a prayer of the faithful which God listens to, bread and wine, fruits of the earth, transformed and shared in the house of the Lord. The liturgy ends with the blessing.[233]

ii. Ps. 124: A Grateful Song of Deliverance

1   If it had not been the LORD who was on our side
    —let Israel now say—

---

[230]   Terrien, *The Psalms*, 475.
[231]   Tate, *Psalms 51-100*, 144.
[232]   See Mays, *Psalms*, 221.
[233]   See Schokel, *Trenta Psalmi*, 288-289.

2   if it had not been the LORD who was on our side
when our enemies attacked us

3   then they would have swallowed us up alive,
when their anger was kindled against us;

4   then the flood would have swept us away,
the torrent would have gone over us;

5   then over us would have gone
the raging waters.

6   Blessed be the LORD,
who has not given us
as prey to their teeth.

7   We have escaped like a bird
from the snare of the fowlers;
the snare is broken,
and we have escaped.

8   Our help is in the name of the LORD;
who made heaven and earth.

a. *Introduction*

Ps. 124 is another example of a communal thanksgiving psalm. A danger is referred to in it, which appears to be of great magnitude and intensity. Various authors have attempted to pinpoint it to a particular event, like the exile or a tempest or the sum of the past dangers faced by Israel. The reference, however, appears to be to something of a general nature.

b. Structure

124:1-5: What might have happened
6-7: Cry of thanks for deliverance
8: Conclusion: affirmation of trust in Yahweh

c. Interpretation

124:1-5: What Might Have Happened

Verses 1-2 form a strong conditional clause and 3-5 the principal clause. A conditional clause is usually more expressive than a real statement. The poet employs herein the technique of repetition, which is a literary or cultic device to emphasise something. The community must share and profess the conviction of the author: "let Israel now say," in other words, "Let Israel repeat it." To be on one's side or "to be with" is a classical formula in the oracles of salvation. It has been beautifully condensed for posterity in the name Emmanuel (*immanu* + *el* = with us + God).

The principal clause (3-5) has three parts:

> If ... then they would have swallowed us up alive
> then the flood would have swept us away
> then over us would have gone the raging waters.

"Fire" and "water" are classical dangers (cf. Isa. 43, 2; Sir 51, 4; Mt. 17, 15). "Fire" is symbolic of the anger of the enemy, and "water" the impetuous arrogance of the enemy. The theological import of the statement is to be taken into consideration. God is present even in these evils and delivers those who seek his help.

124:6-7: Cry of Thanks for Deliverance

In these verses, two vivid images are used: the picture of a wild animal that devours its prey and the snare of the fowler. The community has been saved from these dangers because of God's timely help.

Summing up the psalm, we can say that it captures the original experience of one who was at the point of death and was saved by Yahweh. This experience is applied, by extension, to the whole community. The poem captures within itself an intense religious experience.

d. *Christian Transposition*

1) The psalmist brings home to us the fact of our complete dependence on God.
2) Since God has acted thus in the past, he will continue to do so even in the future.
3) If it were not for God's action in Christ, then death would have swallowed us. Instead, since Jesus has been raised from the dead, we can sing with Paul, "O death, where is your victory?" (1 Cor. 15:55).

III. PSALMS OF LAMENT (PETITION, ENTREATY, SUFFERING)

The largest group of psalms in the Psalter are the psalms of lament. About one-third of the Psalter consists of lament psalms. They are called the "backbone of the Psalter." These are so important that they are viewed as an "imperishable treasure in the Psalter."[234] People in suffering call on God from "out of the depths" (*de profundis*) (Ps. 130:1). This is central to a vital worship.

What are they?

They are cries to God for help raised by people in dire straits. They are protestations rooted in the power of our God to intervene. These perils could be against personal life and well-being. There exists a covenant between Yahweh and the people of God. Because of this relationship, the Lord has a claim on us, both as individuals and as members of the community. Similarly, we also have a claim on the Lord. We have a right to address this God and ask him for a hearing. The Lord has become the God of our problems. This becomes God's problem. That brings about a link between God and us. Lament thus becomes an eloquent appeal to get involved.[235]

The complaints, depending on the dangers, can be divided into individual/personal and communal/national laments.

---

[234] Gunkel, 33.
[235] Craghan, *Psalms,* 99-100.

A. The Lament of an Individual

Ps. 3, 4, 5, 6, 7, 10, 12, 13, 14, 17, 22, 25, 26, 27, 28, 31, 35, 36, 38, 39, 41, 42, 45, 51, 52, 53, 54, 55, 56, 57, 58, 59, 61, 64, 69, 71, 77, 86, 88, 89, 94, 102, 109, 120, 130, 139, 140, 141, 142, 143, 144.

It is a poignant prayer wrung from personal crisis, such as severe sickness or social victimisation, from which the sufferer seeks to be set free. A suppliant puts oneself under the protection of a superior. With symbolic gestures, one admits his/her complete submission and unconditional dependence on him in expressions like "imploring God," "raising one's eyes," "extending one's hands," "prostrating oneself before," "taking refuge in God," and so on. The language and imagery of the laments of an individual are symbolic and stereotypical enough to be applicable to a variety of situations. Patrick D. Miller suggests:

> The search for a readily identifiable situation as the context for understanding the laments may, however, be illusory or unnecessary. The language of these psalms with its stereotypical, generalising, and figurative style is so open-ended that later readers, on the one hand, are stopped from peering behind them to one or more clearly definable sets of circumstances or settings in life, and on the other hand, are intentionally set free to adapt them to varying circumstances and settings.[236]

The troubles and dangers faced by one include i) sickness, ii) enemies, iii) false accusations, and iv) military setting:

---

[236] Patrick D. Miller, Jr., *Interpreting the Psalms* (Philadelphia: Fortress, 1986), 8.

1. The first cause of death and danger of death is illness. Yahweh is the one who sends it and heals it (32:4, 38:2, 69:26, 102:6-10, and 30:2). Illness is a punishment and possesses a purifying character (38:3, 41:4, 107:17). Illness is painted in vivid colours in Ps. 38 and 102. Sickness can bring the threat of death, especially an early and untimely death (102:24).
   The life after death is in *sheol*. It is an enclosed space, like a prison with gates and bars, or like a deep hole or a pit or a well (88:12, 49:19, 30:9, 88:5, 10-12). The descent of the soul into *sheol* means the danger of death (16:9, 30:3, 49:15, 86:13, 89:48).

2. The enemies are those who leave us in the lurch (Ps. 41:5, 7-8). There are three types of enemies: i) friends who become enemies (Book of Job), ii) those who scorn God and take religion lightly (Ps. 69:10-12, 139:21), and iii) adversaries (Ps. 69:26). The sufferers call on God to slay and frustrate their enemies (Ps. 143:9-12).

3. False accusations before a court of law. This is a social injustice. Witnesses may give evidence for one's innocence. One may swear an oath to declare one's justness (Ps. 7:3-5).

4. Some psalms (Ps. 3, 35, 56, 57) have a military setting. The speaker could be a king or a military leader. The military imagery can be metaphorical. The crucial questions in approaching laments include what is wrong with us and who or what are our enemies? This approach opens the way for an explicitly theological understanding of the laments of the individual.

Faced with opponents, the psalmist asserts his innocence in psalms of innocence (7, 17, 26); at other times, he curses his enemies in imprecatory (cursing) psalms (35, 69, 109); and at other times, he acknowledges his guilt and asks forgiveness in penitential psalms (6, 32, 38, 51, 102, 130, 143). One aspect of lament is confidence. Some psalms have the motif of confidence (23).

a. Life Setting (Sitz im Leben)

The original setting of a lament psalm is the worship service. Individual laments are integral liturgical parts of a ritual performed at the request of people suffering from severe ills, especially in cases where an evil spell has been diagnosed as the root of the trouble.[237]

b. Structure

"The plea for help is the one universal prayer emerging from the heart of all those who suffer or are exploited."[238] The following are some elements of the basic structure of an individual's lament: 1) an initial petition explicitly addressed to God: "save me, O God" (Ps. 69:1), 2) a stylised description of the trouble or crisis, 3) an affirmation of trust or confidence in God, 4) a plea or petition for God's response, and 5) a promise or vow to praise God or to offer a sacrifice once the prayer has been answered.[239] Not every element appears in every lament psalm, and there is no fixed order. In some psalms, certain elements are more elaborate and others less. A few of them may even be completely missing in certain psalms. The following is a complete list of the elements:

---

237 Mowinckel, *OT Form Criticism*, 203.
238 J. David Pleins, *The Psalms. Songs of Tragedy, Hope, and Justice* (Maryknoll, NY: Orbis Books, 1993), 16.
239 Allen, *Psalms*, 18; McCann Jr., "The Book of Psalms," 644-646.

i)   Invocation: An appellation to Yahweh and an initial plea (3:1; 6:1; 7:1; 26:1; 38:1; 51:1; 54:1).

ii) Complaint: It can be addressed in three directions: 1) a complaint directed against God (a "you" complaint); 2) a complaint about one's own suffering (an "I" or "we" complaint); or 3) a complaint against the acts of the enemies (a "they" complaint). This is related to existence: self-existence, existence together with others, and existence over against God.[240] The descriptions are vivid and stereotyped (22:1-9, 13-19; 38:1-9, 11-15, 18, 20-21; 69:1b-4, 7-12, 19-21).

iii) Plea/Petition for help: help me; save me; wake up; have mercy, and so on (3:7, 26:11, 57:1, 86:2).

iv) Condemnation of enemies or imprecation against wrongdoers (35:1-8, 69:22-28, 109:6-20).

v)   Affirmation of trust/confidence (13:5, 22:10-11, 31:1-5, 142:5).

vi) Confession of sins or assertion of innocence (26:4-6, 51:5-7).

vii) Acknowledgement of divine response, making a vow or pledge (6:9, 7:17, 56:12, 109:30.

viii) Hymnic elements/blessing (5:4-6, 31:21-24, 69:33-37).

Ps. 7:1-2: Address to God and prayer of petition
3-16: Lament proper:

   3-5: Oath of innocence
   6-8: Petition
   9-16: God saves the good and punishes the wicked

---

240   Claus Westermann, *The Psalms. Structure, Content and Message* (Minneapolis: Augsburg Publishing House, 1980), 37.

17: Promise of thanksgiving

Ps. 13:1-2: Address to God and bitter lament
3-4: Prayer of petition
5-6: Promise of thanksgiving

Ps. 17:1-2: Address to God and a prayer of petition
3-14: The body:

> 3-5: Declaration of innocence
> 6-9: Prayer of petition
> 10-12: Description of the enemy
> 13-14: Moving prayer of petition

15: Expression of trust

Ps. 109:1-2: Preamble (introductory statement)
3-29: Petition
30-31: Conclusion

i.   Psalm 3: Trust in God under Adversity

1   O LORD, how many are my foes!
    many are rising against me;

2   many are saying to me
    "There is no help for you in God."

3   But you, O Lord, are a shield around me
    my glory and the one who lifts up my head,

4   I cry aloud to the LORD,
    and he answers me from his holy hill.

5   I lie down and sleep;

I wake again, for the LORD sustains me.

6 I am not afraid of ten thousands of people
   who have set themselves against me all around.

7 Rise up, O LORD!
   Deliver me, O my God!
   For you strike all my enemies on the cheek;
   you break the teeth of the wicked.

8 Deliverance belongs to the LORD,
   may your blessing be on your people!

a. Introduction

Ps. 3 belongs to the theme-oriented group of prayer songs, traditionally the laments of the individual. It begins with a complaint against the enemies arrayed against him but moves on to a prayer of confidence and assurance of ultimate victory. The language and terminology employed in the psalm have military overtones. It may have been a royal protective psalm. Ps. 3 was regularly used as a morning prayer and Ps. 4 as an evening prayer.[241]

b. Structure

3:1-2:The psalmist complains of his many enemies.
3-6: He expresses his total trust and confidence that
      God will answer his prayer.

---

[241] Craigie, *Psalms 1-50*, 71-72.

7-8: The psalmist requests God to grant victory and feels the certainty of being heard.[242]

c. *Interpretation*

The style of Ps. 3 is dominated by direct address to God: "O LORD, how many are my foes!" (3:1); "You, O LORD, are a shield around me"(3:3); "Rise up, O LORD!" (3:7). This frequent use of direct address to God marks Ps. 3 as a prayer. Verses 1-2 describe the trouble that requires Yahweh's help. Verses 3:3-6 portray the psalmist's confidence in God's eventual delivery. This level of faith is typical in these prayers, and it serves as a guarantee for their future. Verse 3:7 repeats the earlier request, and verse 3:8 praises the Lord and accepts his blessing: "deliverance belongs to the Lord."[243]

Ps. 3:1-2 begins in poetic parallelism, a synonymous parallelism. There is a threefold repetition of "many" in these verses. The first word is "LORD" and the last is "me" in v. 1, and the foes are taking a position between the psalmist and God. The situation in the psalm implies the presence of three personages: the one praying, the Lord, and the group of foes. "My foes, rising against me, saying to me" (1-2a) refer to the enemy. "A shield around me, my glory, the one who lifts up my head" (one who will restore my honour) (3) refers to God. "I lie down, sleep, I wake again" (5) refers to the one praying.

Again the first word in Ps. 3:1-2 is "LORD," and the last is "God." Thus the two references to Lord/God open and close this section. God has the enemies surrounded. The pronoun "I," which begins 3:5, is emphatic, recalling the pronoun "you," which began 3:3,

---

242   Kraus, *Psalms 1-59*, 137.
243   Creach, *Psalms*, 9-10.

and providing a link between the sections 3:3-4 and 3:5-6. The foes presume to stand between the psalmist and God (3:1-2). To signify the inseparability of the psalmist and God, the syntax has changed in 3:3-4 and 3:5-6. Noting the phrases such as the Lord "answers me" (3:4) and "the LORD sustains me" (3:5), John Kselman suggests, "Yahweh and the psalmist are in constant interaction."[244] The foes trust only themselves. The psalmist trusts the one to whom he is inseparably related: "my God" (3:7a). Ps. 3 proclaims that happiness consists of the good news that God's help (v. 8) is forthcoming precisely in the midst of such threats, in order to make life possible (vv. 3-4) and to offer us a peace (v. 5) that the world says is not possible (v. 2).[245]

Verse 3, which introduces three titles or predicates of the Lord, unites 2 and 4 by referring to the call of the one praying and the response of the Lord. Thus, 2-4 present a perfect symmetry. This symmetry extends upwards in the text because the "you" of 3 opposes the enemies of 1-2. It extends downwards because the "I" of 4 prolongs his action into 5. Verse 6 becomes the concrete content of what is said in 4. This experience of the suppliant is extended to the whole people in 8.

A military metaphor is found in the psalm. The suppliant is surrounded by a multitude that encamps around him. He is completely encircled, almost threefold (see the threefold "many" in 1-2). But there is an inner circle between him and the Lord. He is a shield around him, a wall to defend him. Surrounded by the enemy, he peacefully lies down, sleeps, and then wakes up again (5). "Sleep" symbolises tranquility, and "wake up" symbolises the victory of life, which continues.

[244] John S. Kselman, "Psalm 3: A Structural and Literary Study," *CBQ* 49, 1987: 573-580.
[245] McCann Jr., *NIB*, Vol. 4, 693-694.

The morning comes, and the Lord must rise up to save the suppliant by routing the enemy (7). The force of the fist of Yahweh is mentioned, the symbol of God as a warrior. The psalmist's enemies, whose mouths are without teeth, cannot hurt him any more.

d. Christian Transposition

The psalm affirms that "God helps those who cannot help themselves." Is this statement acceptable to the advanced contemporary society, which says, "God helps those who help themselves"? Is this cultural creed in the Bible? Autonomy or self-sufficiency is promoted by some people as the highest virtue.

Prayer is for those who know that they are not self-sufficient. Eugene Peterson says, "Prayer is the language of people who are in trouble and know it, and who believe or hope that God can get them out." He quotes Isaac Bashevis Singer: "I only pray when I am in trouble, but I'm in trouble all the time."[246]

Jesus Christ prayed the psalms. He is the persecuted one, the one who is thrust and cast off into hopeless forsakenness of God. But he is also the one who trusts, who prays, who is united with the Father, who is justified by God, who is arisen. Christians pray Ps. 3 in Christ. The wide scope of expression of the language of the psalm is fulfilled in the reality of Jesus Christ.[247]

---

[246] Eugene A. Peterson, *Answering God: The Psalms as Tools for Prayer* (San Francisco: Harper and Row, 1989), 36; McCann Jr., *NIB*, Vol. 4, 695.

[247] Kraus, *Psalms 1-59*, 143.

ii. Ps. 12: An Assurance of Salvation

1   Help, O LORD, for there is no longer anyone who is godly;
    the faithful have disappeared from humankind;

2   They utter lies to each other;
    with flattering lips and a double heart they speak.

3   May the LORD cut off all flattering lips,
    the tongue that make great boasts.

4   those who say, "With our tongues we will prevail;
    our lips are our own—who is our master?"

5   "Because the poor are despoiled, because the needy groan,
    I will now rise up," says the LORD;
    "I will place them in the safety for which they long."

6   The promises of the LORD are promises that are pure,
    silver refined in a furnace on the ground,
    purified seven times.

7   You, O LORD, will protect us;
    you will guard us from this generation forever.

8   On every side the wicked prowl,
    as vileness is exalted among humankind

a. Introduction

Ps. 12 is symmetrically constructed. It begins with an urgent plea for help (v. 1) and goes on to portray the bad talk of the wicked (v. 2) A petition follows, asking God to destroy the boasters (v. 3). After this comes the arrogant speech uttered by humankind (v. 4). God's utterance of support for the suffering follows (v.

5). God's word is a motive of confidence (v. 6). The psalm concludes with petitions (vv. 7-8).[248] Ps. 12 is a prayer song that incorporates an utterance of God (v. 5). This psalm is a prayer for the Lord's saving help (v. 1) when wickedness is dominant in society. This is a communal lament, which could be interpreted in individual terms, at a time when faithlessness had become rampant in an ancient Israelite community. The psalmist, an ordinary man, who had many a bitter experience of the malice of the wicked in high places (v. 8), goes to the sanctuary for help and receives an assurance from on high (v. 5). He reacts to this assurance and concludes that God's promises are trustworthy (v. 7). The psalm is finely constructed and makes effective use of repetition and contrast. The contrast in speech is between the evil and flattering speech of the wicked (12:1-4) and the pure and true utterances of God (12:5-8).[249]

b. Structure

12:1-4: A unit of plea and complaint
5: The saving word of God
6-8: Expression of confidence and prayer[250]

c. Interpretation

Ps. 12 begins with a supplication that begs for Yahweh's saving intervention (see Ps. 3:7, 6:4, 7:1); good persons appear to have disappeared from the land, and the wicked are rampant. "Help" (1) means "save" (*Yasa* = to be spacious, to be in a spacious locality). Help refers to the possibility of expansion, growth, and development.

---

[248] Juengling, "Psalms 1-41," 847.
[249] Craigie, *Psalms 1-50*, 137.
[250] McCann Jr., *NIB*, Vol. 4, 724.

The "Lord" (YHWH) (1) is the Saviour par excellence (Isa. 43:11, 45:15). "Help" is a request to Yahweh to intervene and exercise on their behalf his salvific activities. The "godly" (1) is one who is dutiful (*hasid, hasidim*: those who remain faithful to Yahweh, do his will in keeping with the covenant, and are devoted to his service). The *godly* are now in danger of being devoured by enemies hostile to God.

Verse 2 indicates the activity of the violent and the persecutors. "Lies" (2): falsehood, emptiness, nothingness. These can also be calumny, slander, malicious gossip, false accusations. "Flattering lips" (2) are lips that utter empty, flattering words. They speak from a "double heart" (2). The heart, in the Hebrew conception, was the seat of the mind. "Double heart" does not indicate the sense "in two minds" (uncertainty); it indicates a double standard and hence implies lies and deceitfulness. They would not speak the truth when a lie would accomplish their goal.[251] In the OT, one can have an evil heart, uncircumcised heart, hardening of heart, a clean heart, new heart, broken heart.

"The tongue that makes great boasts" (3) refers to a tongue that speaks great things. Verse 4 records the arrogant speech of the impious. The wicked boast in their strength. They were saying, "Our lips are with us," against the proper confession "The Lord is with us." Anyone who controls the media controls the market and public opinion: "With our tongue we will prevail": we shall go on speaking insolently; we shall ordinarily utter malicious speech. The "tongue" (4) is an organ of evil speech (Ps. 57:6; 64:4; 140:4, 5, 10). "Who is our master?" (4) is a rhetorical question, with the answer, "No one." The wicked think that they are accountable to no one but themselves. Such an autonomy is the very essence of wickedness.

The focal point of the prophetic liturgy is the message of Yahweh transmitted by the cultic prophet (v. 5) (see Isa. 33:10). Here

---

251   Craigie, *Psalms 1-50*, 138.

we are dealing with a prophetically transmitted statement. The prophetic word says, "I will now rise up." Yahweh intervenes not only because of one suffering individual but "because the poor are despoiled." His action affects the whole people of God. The statement of Yahweh transmitted by the cultic prophet brings salvation to the oppressed and weak. "With this 'now' the manifestation of salvation breaks out into the open in the worst time of adversity, a manifestation that is not still to come but is always present and needs only to becomes active" (Martin Buber).[252] God helps those who cannot help themselves. This good news lies at the heart of Ps. 12.[253] In verse 5, there is a sudden change in lament leading to thanksgiving because of God's action. The violent despoiling of the poor is a social evil that arouses Yahweh to quick and immediate action. The "poor" and "needy" (5) are a special class or group in distress, whose only source of help is Yahweh. "I will now rise up" (5) speaks of an imminent ("now") and salvific action.

Vv. 6-8 deal with the meaning of God's words in v. 5, and this meaning decides and determines everything. The promises of Yahweh are proved and reliable. In contrast to the words of the proud and boastful wicked, the statements of Yahweh are pure and genuine, and everyone can depend on them (v. 6). Like precious metal are the promises of Yahweh, without a trace of anything false or spurious. God keeps his word. V. 7 is a prayer addressed to Yahweh, which extends immediately to the assent given in v. 6. Yahweh's promise of salvation signifies protection for the poor, even when they are surrounded by the wicked and when malice reigns everywhere.[254] Besides the psalmist, others are present in the temple, and the "wicked" are active everywhere (8).

---

[252] Kraus, *Psalms 1-59*, 209-210.
[253] McCann Jr., *NIB*, Vol. 4, 724.
[254] Kraus, *Psalms 1-59*, 210.

d. Christian Transposition

Believers have to suffer persecution, and ungodliness has become prevalent, but they fear little because God is there to come to their rescue. There is a sense of security and assurance available to each one of us.

Ps. 12 goes beyond the fate of an individual. It extends to the distress of the people of God. The words of Yahweh stand in the center of the cultic-prophetic event. Yahweh arises and comes to the help of the helpless. The psalm shows how all things depend on God's word and how reliable and helpful this word actually is.[255]

The church exists now as a minority. In a thoroughly secularised society, we are inclined to accept the credo of the wicked in v. 4 that we are the masters of our own destiny. But as the people of God, we profess to live not according to their words, but by the word of God. We profess that our security lies in God's activity, not our own. We have been sent "into the world," but we "do not belong to the world" (Jn 17:16, 18). Ps. 12 can be heard as a challenge to the church to claim its distinctiveness.[256]

iii. Psalm 22: Plea for Deliverance from Suffering and Hostility

1   My God, my God, why have you forsaken me?
     Why are you so far from helping me, from the words of
     my groaning?

2   O my God, I cry by day, but you do not answer;
     and by night, but find no rest.

---

[255]   Kraus, *Psalms 1-59*, 210-211.
[256]   McCann Jr., *NIB,* Vol. 4, 725.

3   Yet you are holy,
    enthroned on the praises of Israel.

4   In you our ancestors trusted;
    they trusted, and you delivered them.

5   To you they cried, and were saved;
    in you they trusted, and were not put to shame.

6   But I am a worm, and not human;
    scorned by others, and despised by the people.

7   All who see me mock at me;
    they make mouths at me, they shake their heads;

8   "Commit your cause to the LORD; let him deliver—
    let him rescue the one in whom he delights!"

9   Yet it was you who took me from the womb;
    you kept me safe on my mother's breast.

10 On you I was cast from my birth,
    and since my mother bore me you have been my God.

11 Do not be far from me,
    for trouble is near
    and there is no one to help.

12 Many bulls encircle me,
    strong bulls of *Ba'shan* surround me;

13 they open wide their mouths at me,
    like a ravening and roaring lion.

14 I am poured out like water,
    and all my bones are out of joint;

my heart is like wax;
it is melted within my breast;

15 my mouth is dried up like a potsherd,
and my tongue sticks to my jaws;
you lay me in the dust of death.

16 For dogs are all around me;
a company of evildoers encircles me.
My hands and feet have shriveled;

17 I can count all my bones.
They stare and gloat over me;

18 they divide my clothes among themselves,
and for my clothing they cast lots.

19 But you, O LORD, do not be far away!
O my help, come quickly to my aid!

20 Deliver my soul from the sword,
my life from the power of the dog!

21 Save me from the mouth of the lion!
From the horns of the wild oxen you have rescued[257] me.

22 I will tell of your name to my brothers and sisters;
in the midst of the congregation I will praise you:

23 You who fear the LORD, praise him!
all you offspring of Jacob, glorify him;
stand in awe of him all you offspring of Israel!

---

[257] In Hebrew, "answered."

24 For he did not despise or abhor
the affliction of the afflicted;
he did not hide his face from me,
but heard when I cried to him.

25 From you comes my praise in the great congregation;
my vows I will pay before those who fear him.

26 The poor[258] shall eat and be satisfied;
those who seek him shall praise the LORD.
May your hearts live forever!

27 All the ends of the earth shall remember
and turn to the LORD;
and all the families of the nations
shall worship before him.

28 For dominion belongs to the LORD,
and he rules over the nations.

29 To him, indeed, shall all who sleep in the earth bow down;
before him shall bow all who go down to the dust,
and I shall live for him.

30 Posterity will serve him;
future generations will be told about the Lord.

31 And proclaim his deliverance to a people yet unborn,
saying that he has done it.

---

[258] "Poor" or "afflicted" (*anawim*).

a. Introduction

Ps. 22 is a unique psalm. It does not consist of two separate psalms, a lamentation and a thanksgiving, fused into one, but its text is the basis of a liturgy, in which the worshipper moves from lament (22:1-21) to prayer (22:11, 19-21) and finally to praise and thanksgiving (22:22-31).[259] It is an individual lament, a prayer of complaint par excellence, in the context of the community as a whole. Ps. 22 is one of the most touching poetical creations of ancient Israel. The three parties involved in this psalm are God, the individual, and the enemies. The song first leads us into the uttermost depths of suffering. It then soars to the heights of a hymn of praise and thanksgiving. Ps. 22 is the principal OT resource[260] employed by the Gospel evangelists to portray, and to interpret, the climax of Jesus' career, passion, death, and resurrection (they also use Ps. 69 and 31). Jesus used the opening verse of Psalm 22, "My God, my God, why have you forsaken me?" as his prayer on the cross (Mt. 27:46, Mk 15:34). The psalmist, on recovering from his severe illness, went to the temple to perform the ceremony of public thanksgiving, but before the rite, he gave a vivid description of his experience of sickness. This was done to make known to others the wonders God had worked on their behalf. The psalm has been uttered in its entirety in the worship of the cult community (v. 25) after the prayer has been answered (v. 24).[261]

---

259   See Craigie, *Psalms 1-50,* 197.
260   Of the thirteen references to the OT in the passion stories, eight come from the Book of Psalms, and five of these are from Psalm 22.
261   Weiser, *The Psalms,* 219.

b. Structure

      22:1-21a: Distress of abandonment by God
      1-11: Present distress contrasted with God's mercy in the past
      1-10: Forsaken by God and humankind
      1-2: "Why have you forsaken me?"
      3-5: "Yet you are holy"
      6-8: "But I am a worm"
      9-10: "Yet you took me from the womb"
      11: Prayer for help
      12-21a: The enemies of the psalmist

          12-18: Surrounded by trouble
          12-15: "Bulls encircle me"
          16-18: "Dogs around me"
          19-21a: Prayer for deliverance
          21b-31: Praise and thanksgiving for Yahweh's help
          21b: Response from God, a prophetic oracle

      22-26: Thanksgiving, declared by the sufferer
      22-24: "I tell your name to my brothers and sisters"
      25: "My praise in the great congregation"
      26: "The poor shall eat"
      27-31: Universal hymn of praise by the congregation
      27-28: Universal significance of Yahweh's action
      29-31: Reference to posterity

The most distinctive element in the liturgical structure of the psalm is the declaration of trust and confidence by the worshipper at the end of v. 21: "You have answered/rescued me." At the end of the ritual, the worshipper would fulfill his vows (v. 25), both through offering praise to God and through participating in the sacrificial meal (v. 26).[262]

---

[262] Craigie, *Psalms 1-50*, 198; Juengling, "Psalms 1-41," 856; Creach, *Psalms*, 89-90.

c. *Interpretation*

Ps. 22:1-11: This psalm opens with a cry of despair. The sufferer's repeated "My God, my God" for emphasis reveals the intensity of the cry. "My God" refers to the covenantal relationship, a relationship he holds on to and on which he stakes everything. The critical question, "Why, God?" gives vent to the sense of abandonment by God. It is also a protest. We can hear not merely his moans but the desperate, even angry, outcry of the sufferer. He feels the abandonment of God, "forsaken" (v. 1), the distance or absence of God and the silence of God. "Cry" (v. 2) is roaring, like a loud wailing (Ps. 32:3). The feeling of being abandoned by God (vv. 1-2) is contrasted with the holy God "enthroned on the praises of Israel" (v. 3). Yahweh is the object of Israel's activity of praising. It refers to his enthronement through the worship in the temple. Their ancestors placed all their trust in this holy God who rescued them (vv. 4-5). His cry out to God is possible because of his trust in God and the trustworthiness of God. God keeps silence. Therein lies the immense tension from which he suffers.[263]

The poet senses the vast difference between the majesty of God and his own self. In contrast to this God, the sufferer says, "I am a worm, and not human" (v. 6), marred beyond recognition (Job 25:6; Isa. 41:14, 53:3). The one with a lament is despised and mocked at by others (vv. 7-8), because they are convinced that his piety is not genuine and sincere. The real sting of his suffering is the strain on his faith. The attack on his faith evokes in him at the same time new strength. Vv. 9-10 propagate God's solicitude for him. The experience of life as a gift and

---

[263] The contradiction between theology and experience. Theology affirmed unambiguously that trust resulted in deliverance. Experience showed that the God of covenant appeared to have forsaken the worshiper.

the protecting presence of God as all-encompassing from the very moment of birth, felt in the warmth of a mother's breast, provide a basis for renewed expression of trust. In the suffering, the psalmist turns to God and expresses a confession of trust, a motivation for God to intervene on his behalf (vv. 9-10). The affirmation "You have been my God" (v. 10) echoes the cry of v. 1, "My God, my God, why have you abandoned me?" and grounds the apparent contradiction of that sentence in a lifelong relationship with the Lord as a benign father. This section concludes with a petition, v. 11, which is a veritable masterpiece: be not far, but be near because I am in distress and there is no one to help.[264] The awareness of God's nearness in the past (vv. 9-10) is the ground for the present prayer to God to be present and to help. He asks that God be no longer distant.

Ps. 22:12-21a: The language here is specific and vivid, but also metaphorical and open. The two images used here are ravenous animals and the physical agony of sickness.[265] 22:12-18 speak of excruciating suffering. 12-13: Fear of enemies, symbolised by bulls, strong bulls of Bashan,[266] arouses in him once more violent emotions. 14-15: The psalmist uses the strongest language to describe this state of anxiety. His moment of extreme distress is described through figures of speech: he is poured out like water, his bones are out of joint, his heart is melting like wax, and his throat is dried up like a potsherd. This feeling of utter helplessness makes him think that God lays him in the "dust of death" (v. 15). It can be a reference to burial, to which a stretcher, bed, or *sheol* are linked. Here he is confronted with an unsolved

---

264   Juengling, "Psalms 1-41," 856.
265   See Miller, *Interpreting the Psalms*, 105.
266   Bashan is the fertile pasture land east of the Jordan, well known for its strong race of breeding cattle, and the ravening and roaring lion. Lion and ox are conventional pairs to represent the epitome of power. The beast metaphors describe people, the powerful and eminent "enemies of the individual."

mystery. The same God, through whom he expects to be saved, is at work also in his suffering. 16-18: He is unable to get rid of the anxious thoughts that continue to be directed to his enemies and to himself. The thought of imminent death has led the poet to use the illustration of the dogs and robbers dividing his garments. Once dead, his belongings are divided (v. 18). 19-21: The psalmist clings to God, whom he entreats to save his life from the power of his adversaries. That he does not think of vengeance on his enemies makes this psalm specially meaningful for us.[267]

21b-31: Praise and thanksgiving for Yahweh's help. Here we have one of the most effusive and extravagant songs of thanksgiving in the OT. 21b is the sufferer's response, "You have answered/ rescued me," to a prophetic oracle. By means of saying "answered me"/"rescued me," the sufferer declares, "Yahweh has heard me."[268] His confidence is based upon the faith that God would answer his prayers. Vv. 22-26 are references to the performance of a public rite of thanksgiving. 22-24: A congregation (*qahal*) is a gathering of people for a religious purpose (v. 22). God has not ignored or disdained the suffering one, has not "forsaken me" or turned away but has answered him (v. 24). Assured that his prayer has been heard and that God has helped him, he sings a song of thanksgiving. He also invites the congregation to praise God. His deepest need now is to proclaim the glory of God and to have him acknowledged by all. 25-26: The re-establishment of his communion with God is accepted by him as a gift from God himself. In recognition of this fact, he makes his votive offering and invites others to a meal so that they may share in his happiness. "May your hearts live forever" (v. 26) (= "To your health") is a toast to his fellow diners. This will lead them to remember that the God who has come to his help will not forsake their cause either.

267 Weiser, *The Psalms*, 223-224.
268 Kraus, *Psalms 1-59*, 298.

27-28: The psalmist wants not only Israel but also the whole world, all nations (cosmic perspective), to realise the power of Yahweh and bow down before him as their God. 29-31:[269] Everyone—everywhere, of every condition, in every condition—will join in this. Ps. 22:27-31 connects a vision of the universal, comprehensive, everlasting kingdom to what the Lord has wrought in the life of this afflicted one. The knowledge of the "saving acts" of God will be passed on from one generation to another. Through the history of salvation, the belief in God will be propagated throughout the world and throughout the ages.[270] In this thanksgiving song, there are two kinds of movement: first, a movement back and forth between praise (vv. 22-23, 25-26, 27, 29-31a) and reason for praise (vv. 24, 28, 31b); second, creation of a widening circle of praise. The double movement of this song of thanksgiving has two effects: a movement from the deepest depths of agony to the highest heights of praise to God and a movement outwards, a wave of praise from God's deliverance of this one person. The constant struggle between despair and trust has ended in the dominance of trust, vindicated by the answer of God.[271]

d. Christian Transposition

Ps. 22 is an expression of that primal outcry of human suffering that we hear in the OT and in our own experience. In the NT, this psalm provides the primary interpretive clues to the meaning of the passion and death of Christ. His resurrection does tell us that God is at cross-purposes with suffering, fully present in it, and at work to overcome it.[272] When he felt forsaken by God,

---

[269] Some scholars contend that vv. 29-31 is a later addition.
[270] See Weiser, *The Psalms*, 224-226.
[271] See Miller, *Interpreting the Psalms*, 108.
[272] Ibid., 108-110.

Jesus remained faithful by uttering the opening words of the psalm. Guided by the psalm, Jesus entered upon the way that led him through his most bitter passion, but ended in the triumph of faith and in the victory of the kingdom of God. Thus Ps. 22 has been used in the NT in the sense of a messianic prophecy, pointing to the consummation of the rule of God in Christ.[273]

Jesus identifies himself in his passion and death with the suffering and dying. He can offer comfort to those of us who walk now where the psalmist walked. The transition at v. 21b is now understood not in deliverance *from* death, as was the case for the psalmist, but in deliverance *through* death, achieved in the resurrection of Jesus. And it is that deliverance that is the ground of praise, both for the sufferer (vv. 22-26) and for the "great congregation" (vv. 27-31).[274]

Ps. 22:1a is quoted by Jesus on the cross (Mk 15:34, Mt. 27:46). This psalm figures prominently in the passion story (v. 18 in Mk 15:24, v. 7 in Mk 15:29; Mt. 27:35, Mt. 27:39, v. 8 in Mt. 27:43; Jn 19:24, v. 15 in Jn 19:28; Lk. 23:34). By telling the story of Jesus using Ps. 22, the Gospel writers affirm that in Jesus' faithful suffering, as in the psalmist's faithful suffering, God was present. God's presence with the afflicted and dying opens up new possibilities for understanding and living human life, as well as for understanding and accepting death.[275]

In its unity, Ps. 22 provides a scenario for reflection on the significance of Jesus' death and resurrection that is different from the traditional models of sacrifice, trial, and combat. The psalm interprets Jesus' passion and death as a theodicy for those who commit their way to the Lord. The psalm interprets Jesus'

---

[273] Cf. Weiser, *The Psalms*, 226.

[274] See Craigie, *Psalms 1-50*, 203.

[275] See McCann Jr., *NIB*, Vol. 4, 762, 766.

passion and resurrection as a summons to the world to believe in the reign of the Lord.

The psalm suggests that we think of the Lord's Supper as a thanksgiving of the lowly. It is the Eucharist instituted and defined by a lowly one and shared by the lowly.[276]

When Jesus in the agony of the cross prays the first words of Ps. 22, two things happen: 1) He enters the archetypal affliction of abandonment by God, which was experienced in the OT by those who prayed Ps. 22 and which is described in surpassing words and images. This means that Jesus solidly identifies himself with the entire fullness of suffering. The path of the Son of man coming from heaven leads to the lowest depths of misery. 2) The first Christian community now saw associations between the fate of the OT petitioner in Ps. 22 and the death of Jesus on the cross.[277]

Cross and glory, death and resurrection, are like two sides of the came coin: "my God, my God" (v. 1) and "I will tell of your name" (v. 22).

iv. Psalm 51: Prayer for Cleansing and Pardon

1   Have mercy on me, O God
    according to your steadfast love;
    according to your abundant mercy
    blot out my transgressions.

2   Wash me thoroughly from my iniquity
    and cleanse me from my sin.

---

[276]   Mays, *Psalms,* 114-115.
[277]   Kraus, *Psalms 1-59,* 301.

3   For I know my transgressions,
    and my sin is ever before me.

4   Against you, you alone, have I sinned,
    and done what is evil in your sight,
    so that you are justified in your sentence
    and blameless when you pass judgment.

5   Indeed, I was born guilty,
    a sinner when my mother conceived me.

6   You desire truth in the inward being;
    therefore teach me wisdom in my secret heart.

7   Purge me with hyssop, and I shall be clean;
    wash me, and I shall be whiter than snow.

8   Let me hear joy and gladness;
    let the bones that you have crushed rejoice.

9   Hide your face from my sins,
    and blot out all my iniquities.

10 Create in me a clean heart, O God,
    and put a new and right spirit within me.

11 Do not cast me away from your presence,
    and do not take your holy spirit from me.

12 Restore to me the joy of your salvation,
    and sustain in me a willing spirit.

13 Then I will teach transgressors your ways,
    and sinners will return to you.

14 Deliver me from bloodshed, O God,

O GOD of my salvation,
and my tongue will sing aloud of your deliverance.

15 O Lord, open my lips,
and my mouth will declare your praise

16 For you have no delight in sacrifice.
If I were to give a burnt offering, you would not be pleased.

17 The sacrifice acceptable to God is a broken spirit;
a broken and contrite heart, O God, you will not despise.

18 Do good to Zion in your good pleasure;
rebuild the walls of Jerusalem,

19 then you will delight in right sacrifices,
in burnt offerings and whole burnt offerings;
then bulls will be offered on your altar.

a. Introduction

"Ps. 51 stands out in the Psalter. Its peak statements are unique. And its fullness is incomprehensible."[278] It is the most profound confession of sin in the Bible and one of the most moving prayers in the OT. It is an individual lament for help, the most important or the best known of the seven Penitential Psalms (6, 32, 38, 51, 102, 130, 143). Ps. 51 is the fullest exposition of the simple confession in the OT: "I have sinned." The worshipper's spiritual affliction is made to occupy the very center of the psalm. This psalm contains the sharpest and most complete expression of the penitential theme. It has had an incalculable influence on the theology and practice of the Christian faith. The religious ideas of the psalm are more related

---

[278] Kraus, *Psalms 1-59*, 5-7.

to the concepts of the seventh and sixth centuries BC. The poem may well be the writer's expression of his own consciousness of sin and the need for forgiveness. Physical suffering is connected with guilt in the OT. Ps. 51 was used in Israel as a general penitential prayer. Instead of material sufferings, the worshipper's spiritual affliction is made to occupy the very center of the psalm.

"Ps. 51 is found all through the history of the church and Christian spirituality. It forms the underlying plan of the *Confessions* of St. Augustine. It is loved, meditated, and commented on by Gregory the Great. It was the battle cry for Joan of Arc's soldiers. It was studied acutely by Martin Luther, who wrote unforgettable pages on it. It is the hidden mirror of conscience for the characters of Dostoievsky and is the key to his novels."[279] This prayer starts with a consideration of ourselves and the consciousness of our sins and rises finally to contemplation of God by way of our neighbour.

b. Structure

51:1-9: The reign of sin

1-2: Address to God and prayer of petition
3-6: Confession of guilt and motives for God's response
7-9: Actual prayer for deliverance from sin

10-17: The reign of grace

10-12: Prayer for a clean heart and a willing spirit
13-17: Praise and thanksgiving

18-19: A later liturgical addition

---

279   Martini, *What Am I*, 83.

c. Date

In its original form, it dates back to the pre-exilic times. The earliest date for the psalm in its present form is post-exilic. It could be dated between Ezekiel and Nehemiah.[280]

d. Interpretation

Ps. 51 is divided into two sections: 1-9: the sphere of sin and 10-17: the sphere of grace.

51:1-9: The Reign of Sin

In this section, there is a sort of obsessive presence of words related to sin, a presence that envelops and dominates the whole section. It is another way of saying, "I have my sin always before me." This part of the psalm focuses on confession of sin. It also recognises the divine power to cleanse from guilt and the need for God's mercy. In contrast to this, there are three pairs of nouns, namely, i) that which God possesses: "steadfast love and abundant mercy" (1); ii) that which human beings desire: "truth and wisdom" (6); and iii) that which they ask of God: "joy and gladness" (8).

51:1-2: Address to God and Prayer of Petition

Ps. 51 begins with a focus on God. The psalm appeals to the goodness and mercy of Yahweh and begins with "have mercy." The plea appeals to God's steadfast love and abundant mercy. "Steadfast love" (*hesed*) (1) refers to God's gracious, self-giving character and reliable covenant promises leading to "covenant loyalty." "Mercy" (*hanan*) (gracious), "abundant

---

[280] Kraus, *Psalms 1-59*, 501.

mercy" (*rahamim*) (1) is a feeling similar to what a mother feels for her baby (motherly compassion) or a brotherly/sisterly feeling for others, that is, one's deepest feeling for another person. The prayer seeks a cleansing and purification from all "transgressions," "iniquity," and "sin." "Blot out" (1) implies his deep desire for restoration of his broken relationship with God. "Iniquity" (2) is a deviation from the right path, a deliberate act, not an accidental wrongdoing.[281] It involves the personal guilt or culpability of the sinner. "Transgressions" (1) suggests willful rebellion. The petitioner is pleading for a thorough cleansing of his guilt. It must be eliminated totally. In this section, there is a complete forfeiture of self, on the one hand, and a desperate trust in God, on the other.

51:3-6: Confession of Sin and Profound Realisation of Its Nature

These verses deal with the recognition of one's own sin. Those who confess their sins know and believe that their life is judged by God. This is the point of verses 3 and 4. The root idea of "sin" is "missing the mark" (Judg. 20:16b). The failure involved is the result of choice or of a clear act of will. In Ps. 51, we can see a process leading from disorientation to orientation. Sin is a disruption of the relationship between God and the individual. Verse 4 is a way of saying that apart from God's relation to all human acts, there would be no sin. Sins against others are really sins against God. The psalmist makes a straightforward acknowledgement of his sin (51:4). The author is simply saying, "You, God, are in the right; I am in the wrong."[282] In 4a, there is what we call a biblical *rib* pattern. It is a technical term in OT studies for the complaint that one member of a covenant (Yahweh/Prophet) issues against the offending member. This

---

[281] Anderson, *Psalms,* Vol. 1, 391-393.

[282] Kevin Perrotta, *Psalms. An Invitation to Prayer* (Chicago: Loyola Press, 2000), 46.

is sometimes called a "prophetic lawsuit" or "covenant lawsuit." Here God forms the offended party. "Against you, you alone, have I sinned" (4). A posterior application of it has been made to David: his sin against Uriah (2 Sam. 11-12). In 4b, the stress is not on the justice of the judge but on the innocence of one member in the rib pattern. The psalmist does not appeal to the justice that ought to condemn the guilty but to the mercy that pardons the penitent.

The presence of acts that are "transgressions," "iniquity," "sin" (1-3) reveals something more deeply rooted in people: one's sinful condition. To express this condition, the Hebrews went back to their origin, to their birth or, still further, to the moment of conception (5) (cf. Isa. 48:8, Hos. 12:2, Ps. 58:3). The idea here is not that matrimony is something sinful, but that humans are born into a world full of sin.[283] The environment in which a child grows up is already saturated with sin and temptation. The poet's thoughts penetrate to the ultimate cause of every sin. He realises that the profound relations between sin and human nature operate in his own life. The emphasis is on the sin of the sinner, not on the sinner's mother or on the act of conception itself. "Inward being" (6) refers to the innermost parts of humans. God works in these parts that they may acquire "wisdom," which consists of openness to God and dependence on God.

51:7-9: Actual Prayer for the Forgiveness of Sins

"Hyssop" (7) was a small bushy plant. Cleansing power was attributed to the shrub as such, and it also functioned as a sprinkler. It was employed as a symbol of that inward cleansing that only God could effect.[284] V. 8 anticipates the second part

---

[283] Anderson, *Psalms,* 395.
[284] Hyssop, a caper plant, was used at the first Passover (Ex. 12:24) for the sprinkling of the lintels and door posts of the Hebrew homes;

of the psalm. When God pronounces the sentence of pardon, it will be joyful news, and even his bones will rejoice. "Gladness" and "rejoice" are synonyms of joy. "Bones" (8) may denote one's personality or self. In v. 9, the imperatives and the images underline the aspect of sin. The guilt stands between Yahweh and the petitioner. May God "blot out" that which is intolerable, that which separates us from him.

51:10-17: The Reign of Grace

51:10-12: Prayer for a Clean Heart and a Willing Spirit

A radical change is visible in the second part. In vv. 10-12, the psalmist prays for a new creation in his depraved inner self. "Who can bring a clean thing out of an unclean? No one can" (Job 14:4). There is need for creating something new, and only God can create anything. The psalmist cries out, "Create in me a clean heart, O God" (51:10). Only God's independent, creative act can renew a person's heart. The heart in the OT "simply denotes the center of human existence as the seat of all feeling, thinking, and willing, the spirit refers to the effective power emanating from Yahweh that pervades all feeling, thinking, and will."[285] In 10-12, there is a threefold calling on the spirit (cf. Gen. 1). It is a request to the spirit to re-create the penitent. He cannot raise himself to the sphere of grace. It has to be through an action of God, through a gift of God. The spirit is i) a "right spirit" (10): a steadfast spirit; ii) "a holy spirit" (11): a spirit that makes the penitent live in the divine or holy sphere; and iii) a "willing spirit" (12): a spirit that denotes spontaneous initiative, generosity in difficulties, one who desires to receive a new

---

in later times it was used to cleanse lepers (Lev. 14) as well as in the purification of one defiled by contact with a corpse (Num. 19). Anderson, *Psalms*, 397; Tate, *Psalms 51-100*, 21.

[285] Kraus, *Psalms 1-59*, 505.

dynamism.[286] The "Holy Spirit" appears in the OT only in Ps. 51:11 and Isa. 63:10-11.

In short, a spirit that proceeds from God is steadfast and willing, becomes a dynamic impulse for human action, and will really produce a new creature from the sinful person. The spirit is the inner power that lies behind all action. "Do not take your holy spirit from me" (11) means do not allow him to lose the election or to be rejected, as shown in its parallel "Do not cast me away from your presence" (cf. 2 Kgs 13:23; the opposite 2 Kgs 17:20, 24:20).

51:13-17: Praise and Thanksgiving

This section contains a vow (v. 13), petitions (vv. 14-15), and thoughts about the right, God-pleasing sacrifice (vv. 16-17). Already transformed, the suppliant can dedicate himself to preaching conversion (13). The theme of the first part, sin and iniquity, resounds here in an indirect way, this time bringing salvation. "Bloodshed" (14) refers to homicide and, in a wide sense, any violence. The psalmist is asking to be delivered from the above guilt. When applied to David, it can refer to the assassination of Uriah. Liberated from grave fault, the psalmist can intone the praise of God (cf. 14b, 35:28, 71:24). The praise loosens up the tongue, the lips, and the mouth (v. 15).

In vv. 16-17, the thought about the right offering has an opposition between ritual sacrifices and "a broken spirit and contrite heart." These are metaphors for the mind and will made humble by God's judgment upon the sinner. Underlying v. 16 is the prophetic critique of sacrifice and favours personal commitment and transformation. Verses 16 and 17 are composed of a kind of pattern: "not this but the other" (relative negation). God's supposed disinterest in animal sacrifice may be an indication that temple worship is now no longer

---

[286] Tate, *Psalm 51-100*, 31.

possible; all that can now be offered is a "broken spirit." Sacrifices are nothing in comparison with a broken heart (Ps. 40:6-7). "A broken and contrite heart" denotes a way of life of people characterised by humility and openness to offer themselves to God.

Verses 18-19 are additions, an actualisation of the psalm after the exile. The exile was a time to make the heart contrite through penance. Now the time for pardon and reconciliation has come (cf. Isa. 40:2). In the new conditions, the sacrifices will have value. Now they return to "Zion"; "walls of Jerusalem" (18) point to the final epoch of the exile. "Right sacrifices" (19) refer to the traditional ones. "Bulls" (19) refer to costly sacrifices. These verses remind us of the fact that sin is never simply a matter of individual decisions; it is also a matter of corporate, institutionalised evil.

e.   Christian Transposition

Ps. 51 reminds us of a perennial feature of the human situation: sin. Israel's history is a long list of mistakes. This psalm is not merely about Israel, or David, or some unknown ancient psalmist; it is also about us. It is embarrassing to admit that sin pervades our lives as individuals, families, and churches. Ps. 51 also contains good news about God's nature. God is willing to forgive sinners and is able to re-create people. Sin is a powerful and persistent reality, but God's power is a more enduring reality. With God's grace, a disobedient people become partners of an eternal covenant. With God's grace, incapable disciples of Jesus turn the world upside down (Acts 17:6). With God's grace, a former persecutor of the Christians and Christ becomes an ambassador to preach Christ's Gospel to the Gentiles. This is the good news.[287]

---

[287]   McCann Jr., *NIB*, Vol. 4, 887-888.

Jesus went further than the psalmist. He taught us to call God our Father. Like the prodigal son, we too must recognise and acknowledge our sinfulness as we approach our compassionate Father. As we pray, "Forgive us our trespasses as we forgive those who trespass against us," we express our desire to forgive all who have harmed us.[288]

A Christian is entirely dependent on the merciful activity of God. Only God can give us the pardon of our sins. He alone can break the barriers that make a separation between God and human beings and blot out what is intolerable. Only by God's creative, renewing power can the heart be cleansed and led to a new obedience. Our future is also in the hands of God. Everything is God's act.

Ps. 51 makes us see our sinfulness as a personal affront to our God. In sinning, we also hurt our brothers and sisters; we must take steps to overcome the pain we have caused them. Covenant links our God and our community with our individual actions. To pray Ps. 51 is to assume the ministry of reconciliation.[289]

Through Jesus, the Spirit does indeed heal our hearts. Ps. 51, Jer. 31:33, and Ezra 36:26 taught Israel to expect that when God brought his kingdom, he would make their hearts new by his Spirit. Through Jesus, by the power of his Spirit, God is indeed ready to make us new.

"There is a strong connection between social and political reconciliation and conversion of heart . . . . There is no conversion of heart that does not reach out into social and political reconciliation."[290]

---

[288] David E. Rosage, *The Lord Is My Shepherd. Praying the Psalms* (Ann Arbor, MI: Servant Books, 1984), 79-80.

[289] Craghan, *Psalms*, 115.

[290] Martini, *What Am I*, 82.

B.   National (Communal) Psalms of Lament

The emphasis is on the covenant, God's mighty acts in their nation's history, of his present and future judgment, of salvation.

a.   *Setting (Sitz im Leben)*

National days of prayer and penance, days of favours bestowed on Israel (44:1). It is almost Yahweh's business to help them (74:2, 80:15).

b.   *Structure*

Similar to what is given for the individual psalms of lament:

> 79:1-4: Call upon God and lament
> 5-12: Prayer of petition
> 13: Conclusion
>
> 137:1-3: Lament over the afflictions of exile
> 5-6: Lament over the mockery of oppression
> 7-9: Curse against Babylon and Edom

i.   Ps. 60: Prayer for National Victory after Defeat (cf. Ps. 108:6-13)

1   O God, you have rejected us, broken our defences;
   you have been angry; now restore us!

2   You have caused the land to quake; you have torn it open;
   repair the cracks in it, for it is tottering.

3   You have made your people suffer hard things;
you have given us wine to drink that made us reel.

4   You have set up a banner for those who fear you,
to rally to it out of bowshot.

5   Give victory with your right hand, and answer us,
so that those whom you love may be rescued.

6   God has promised in his sanctuary:
"With exultation I will divide up She'chem,
and portion out the Vale of Suc'coth,

7   Gil'ead is mine, and Manas'seh is mine;
E'phraim is my helmet;
Judah is my scepter.

8   Mo'ab is my washbasin;
on E'dom I hurl my shoe;
over Philis'tia I shout in triumph

9   Who will bring me to the fortified city?
who will lead me to E'dom?

10 Have you not rejected us, O God?
You do not go out, O God, with our armies.

11 O grant us help against the foe,
for human help is worthless.

12 With God we shall do valiantly;
it is he who will tread down our foes.

a. Introduction

Ps. 60 is a natural lament of ancient Israel, occasioned by a defeat in battle, whose time and place remain unknown. The traditions regarding holy war (or *jihad*) are presupposed here. For the Israelites, wars are a religious affair; they are a part of their life in accord with the covenant stipulations. For this reason, the ark—a war palladium: an object on which the safety of something is regarded as bound up—was carried by sacred personnel to the scene of battle (1 Sam. 4:5). The army is led by Yahweh, the mighty warrior (Ps. 24:8). He is supposed to dwell in the camp with the army (Dt 23:14, Judg. 4:14). A common battle cry is "Yahweh is a man of war" (Ex. 15:3) or "A sword for Yahweh and for Gideon" (Judg. 7:20). In other words, Yahweh himself wields the sword and grants victory to his people. Hence the actual number of soldiers never mattered (Judg. 7:2-8). The climax of a *jihad* is the mysterious, sudden, and numinous terror or panic or fright that the Lord would send upon the foes, who would be utterly confounded and bring about their ruin (Josh. 10:10, Judg. 4:15, 1 Sam. 7:10). A defeat would be because Yahweh is not leading the army, and they would lament for it (66:10, 44:9). It is in the light of the traditions regarding the holy war that we have to view the reactions consequent on a defeat, the reactions admirably summed up in Ps. 60.

b. Structure

60:1-5: Invocation and lament
6-8: Divine oracle
9-12: Expression of confidence and trust in God

c. Interpretation

60:1-5: Invocation and Lament

A defeat in battle means that the Lord has rejected Israel (Ps. 89:38). "Restore us" (1): rally us, take us into your power. He made the land to "quake" (2). Verses 1-2 outline the military disaster with the help of conventional vocabulary the Israelites were wont to employ while describing a man's reaction to an announcement of bad news: he is shaken with emotion, becomes weak, is physically broken, and he totters and falls to the ground. He has set a "banner" (*nes*) (4): a standard, ensign, signal. It is not a rallying point but an order to flee. "Those whom you love" (5) are the soldiers who have fled from the battlefield and thus saved their lives. "Your right hand" is a symbol of God's irresistible power and the instrument he uses to save his people (Ex. 15:6, 12).

60:6-8: Divine Oracle

"Sanctuary" (*quodaesh*) (6) implies apartness, sacredness, holiness. It is not the Jerusalem temple but the celestial sanctuary where Yahweh has his abode. "Divide up" denotes division as well as allotment to individual tribes (Josh. 13:7, 18:10, 19:51; 1 Kgs 18:6). "Portion out": Yahweh, claiming, in virtue of conquest rights, the whole land of Palestine, as his "Shechem" is in central Palestine (Israelite settlements in the west). "Succoth" is in trans-Jordan (Israelite settlements in the east). "Gilead" (7) is in the east, and the others in the west. All these, once part of David's kingdom, are now claimed by God as his own. "Helmet" means a place of safety, of protection. "Scepter" (ref. to the oracle of Judah: Gen. 49:10) can be the mace: the rod with a round head of stone or metal, part of the royal equipment and an instrument of war. "Moab," "Edom," and "Philistia" (8) are three pagan countries to the east, south, and west. They stand for the "greater Canaan," which obviously belongs to Yahweh. "Washbasin" can be an allusion to the Dead Sea, on the service to Israel. "Hurl my shoe" refers to Edom as a stool on which Yahweh rests his feet (Ps. 110:1, Josh. 10:24). It implies effective and active possession. "Shout in triumph": the shout or cry victors in battle were wont to emit.

60:9-12: Expression of confidence and trust in God

"Fortified city" (9) could be Bozrah, the rocky, craggy, impregnable capital of the Edomites. The first person in this verse could refer to the king. "Do valiantly" (12): achieve might, make a display of strength. "Tread down" can refer to the custom of the victor's laying his foot upon the neck of the prostrate foe.

d. Christian Transportation

Israel is often in distress, which is attributed as a punishment for their sinfulness. In this context, they had recourse to God in confidence and humility. Ps. 60 is a prayer of God's people in distress.

In the NT, there is reference to the interval between the resurrection of Christ and his *parousia,* characterised by suffering. Ps. 60 can thus be appropriated by us. It is a prayer of the church on earth between the two comings of Christ.

ii. Ps. 115: The Importance of Idols and the Greatness of God

1 Not to us, O Lord, not to us, but to your name give glory, for the sake of your steadfast love and your faithfulness.

2 Why should the nations say,
   "Where is their God?"

3   Our God is in the heavens,
    he does whatever he pleases.

4   Their idols are silver and gold,
    the work of human hands.

5   They have mouths but do not speak;
    eyes, but do not see.

6   They have ears. But do not hear;
    noses, but do not smell.

7   They have hands, but do not feel;
    feet, but do not walk;
    they make no sound in their throats.

8   Those who make them are like them;
    so are all who trust in them.

9   O Israel, trust in the LORD!
    He is their help and their shield.

10 House of Aaron, trust in the LORD!
    He is their help and their shield.

11 You who fear the LORD, trust in the LORD!
    He is their help and their shield.

12 The LORD has been mindful of us; he will bless us;
    he will bless the house of Israel;
    he will bless the house of Aaron;

13 he will bless those who fear the LORD,
    both small and great.

14 May the LORD give you increase,
both you and your children.

15 May you be blessed by the LORD,
who made heaven and earth.

16 The heavens are the LORD's heavens,
but the earth he has given to human beings,

17 The dead do not praise the LORD,
nor do any that go down into silence

18 But we will bless the LORD
from this time on and forevermore.
Praise the LORD!

a. Introduction

This psalm needs to be read in sequence with Ps. 114 (MT 114-115 = LXX 113). In the Breviary there is 113a and b.

b. Structure

115:1-2: Address/petition and lament
3-8: Satire on idols
9-11: Exhortation to trust
12-15: Blessing
16-18: Response

Look first at 9-11, the central part of the psalm. In it, the people accept the covenant that is proposed to them. This adhesion is introduced by v. 8, which is a conclusion of 5-7, which is introduced by 3-4, which reply to the question in v. 2. Verses 9-11 are prolonged on the other side by 12-13, which recalls the benediction pronounced by 14-15. This benediction produces an explosion of joy (16-18).

c. Interpretation

115:1-2: Address/Petition and Lament

Ps. 114 recalls the marvels of Yahweh. In Ps. 115, the assembly is conscious of becoming proud and asks God to rectify and purify their intentions (1). The rhetorical question (2) wants to affirm: After all that Yahweh has done for us, the pagans are mad to believe that our God is powerless.

115:3-8: Satire on Idols

Verse 3 is a response to the question in 2: "Our God is in the heavens." "In the heavens" is not a synonym for heaven, but refers to God's divine transcendence. He is not powerless, because he does whatever he pleases. It does not deal with some sort of whim but refers to his design of love. Verse 4 is a description of the idols of the pagans. 5-7 is a mocking denunciation of the powerlessness of the gods. Their incapacity to speak (5a and 7c) is the greatest sign of their nonexistence. What a difference from God, whose word has brought forth the world and gave life to a people. Verse 8 is a sort of imprecation on the idolaters. It is calling upon them, as punishment, the very lot of the idols: nonexistence (5-7), spiritual death.

115:9-11: Exhortation to Trust

The people are invited to put their faith in Yahweh, a faith that is to be refused to the idols.

1) The Levites address successively "Israel," "house of Aaron" (priests), and those "who fear the Lord" (the

whole people). They are covenant partners (Dt 29:9-10, Josh. 9:33, 2 Kgs 23:2).

2) "Trust in the Lord": manifest your trust in Yahweh entering into his alliance.

3) "He is their help and shield": the reply of each of the groups mentioned. In Hebrew, this third person is equal to the first person plural.

4) "Shield" is used for Yahweh always in the context of the alliance. It is, perhaps, a way of indicating the (stronger) partner in a covenant who is engaged in providing the other protection.

115:12-15: Blessing

12, 13: Israel has entered the covenant once again. Only man's part is visible, but the real actor is God. The names are once again recalled, probably to show that each group will be blessed and also to show the abundance of the blessing.

14-15: the blessing of Yahweh. The blessing, most desired, is growth in the number of descendants (14). Verse 15 is a formula of blessing.

16-18 is a kind of pendant to 1-8. God had confided the earth to humans to work on it and make it productive. The Hebrew word for "earth" can mean a country, the Promised Land. "Go down into silence" (17): to sheol. The transcendence of Yahweh and the gift of the land lead to giving praise.

d. Christian Transposition

Father, creator and ruler of heaven and earth, you made human beings in your likeness to subdue the earth and master it, and to recognise the work of your hands in created beauty. Grant that your children, thus surrounded on all sides by signs of your presence, may live continually in Christ, praising you through him and with him.

iii. Ps. 123: Supplication for Mercy

1 To you I lift up my eyes
 O you who are enthroned in the heavens!

2 As the eyes of servants
 look to the hand of their master,
 as the eyes of a maid to the hands of her mistress,

 so our eyes look to the LORD our God,
 until he has mercy upon us.

3 Have mercy upon us, O LORD, have mercy upon us,
 for we have had more than enough contempt.

4 Our soul has had more than its fill
 of the scorn of those who are at ease,
 of the contempt of the proud.

a. *Introduction*

The context of Ps. 123 is that of a nation exposed to contempt and scorn of arrogant adversaries, rising from the overlordship of Persia after the exile and from internal conflicts. This psalm is one of the finest examples of piety, expressed in simple, truthful, natural, and sincere prayer. One's eyes are fixed on God, like the eyes of a slave on the hand of his master, that he may have mercy because we are scorned.

b. Structure

123:1-2: Expression of confidence
3-4: Petition and lament

c. Interpretation

123:1-2: Expression of Confidence

In this section, there is a change of style from a personal prayer (1) to that of the community (2): "my eyes" and "our eyes." In v. 1, there is humble submission and trust in Yahweh. God is the only one who can save us. The picture in v. 2 expresses reverential awe, submission, and humility, on one hand, and it expresses devoted love and trustful hope in the fatherly care of God, on the other hand. When these two attitudes are combined, there is a genuine attitude of prayer.

123:3-4: Petition and Lament

The worshipper and community suffer grievously from the contempt of the proud oppressors. Their desire to become better is concretised and takes the form of a prayer for mercy. The supplicant does not appeal to his rights or merits. He does not put his trust in himself but only in God. This person seeks God's help because Israel had more than enough of contempt. "Those who are at ease and the proud" (4) are those who grant only scorn. Those who are at ease, negative value (Isa. 32:9, Amos 6:1, Zech. 1:15), are those who despise or humiliate the others. The humiliating attitude can be found at deferent levels on the social scale. The arrogant can be the subordinates. The psalm could have been applied to foreign overlords from Persia or Syria (Isa. 26:13).

The suppliant does not approach God with demands but with faith; he does not impose terms but waits. Such a person can always expect mercy from God, and he will never be humiliated.

d. Christian Transposition

A characteristic example is found in the Gospels: the Pharisee and the tax collector (Lk. 18:8-14). The tax collector does not dare to lift up his eyes to heaven. The Pharisee is at ease because of his own works. He is good and despises the others, the non-observant.

Is the spirituality of slavery a Christian element? (Rom. 8:15). The point of comparison is not fear or servility but abandonment and dependence. If everything is God's mercy or grace, then the humiliating human differences are overcome.

IV. WISDOM PSALMS

a. What Is Wisdom Literature?

It is concerned with training people to succeed, to live a good life. The method used in it is observation. The form used by it is maxims. Wisdom literature has a secular character.

b. Wisdom Psalms

There are psalms that make free use of the language and ideas present in the wisdom literature. Some of these fall into the category of the wisdom psalms, and other psalms have wisdom influences present in them.

i. Style

The following are styles present in them:

- *Makarisms* (blessings) (1:1, 112:1)
- Numerical sayings (62:11)
- Proverbial sayings (37:16.21; cf. Prov. 15:16)
- Exhortations (37:1-8)
- An acrostic arrangement: the first letters of successive lines or strophes
- Appear in alphabetic order (25, 34, 37, 111, 112, 119)
- An anthological style: no connection between the sayings (119; cf. Book of Proverbs)

ii. Themes

- Fate of the good and the evil (Ps. 1)

- Retribution prosperity of the wicked and suffering of the righteous (37, 49, 73)
- Fear of the Lord (128)
- Reverence for the *Torah* (1, 19b, 119)

"Wisdom psalms . . . are substantially molded by a characteristic language, the reflective mood and the didactic intention and the imagery, topics, and motives of Israel's sages, whoever they were" (*OT Form Criticism*, 220).

c. Life Setting (*Sitz im Leben*)

It is said that with Ben Sira, the Israelite sages became worshippers. The wisdom psalms have a diadactic (sapiential) and cultic setting.

i. Ps. 1: The Two Ways

1 Happy are those
   who do not follow the advice of the wicked,
   or take the path that sinners tread,
   or sit in the seat of scoffers;

2 but their delight is in the law of the LORD,
   and on his law they meditate day and night.

3 They are like trees
   planted by streams of water,
   which yield their fruit in its season
   and their leaves do not wither.
   In all that they do, they prosper.

4 The wicked are not so
   but are like chaff that the wind drives away.

5   Therefore the wicked will not stand in the judgment
     nor sinner in the congregation of the righteous;

6   for the LORD watches over the way of righteous,
     but the way of the wicked will perish.

a. Introduction

Ps. 1 is a vivid and graphic description of the ways of life of the righteous and the unrighteous. The psalmist dwells upon the lot Yahweh has in store for the two groups, and then he brings his considerations to a close with a spirited confession of faith. This psalm is usually called either a wisdom song or a *Torah* psalm (one dealing with the *Torah*; cf. Ps. 1:2). It probably originated during the Second Temple period (fourth and third century BC). The author is a sage.

The background of the psalm is the situation after the Babylonian exile, when the Jews were surrounded by pagans, with the consequent temptations to follow their gods. The priests were negligent (Mal. 1:78), and the Levites deserted the temple. The faithful clergy and sages instructed the people, probably, during the solemn feasts. Ps. 1 arose in such an occasion. It was connected with the cult.

b. Structure

> 1:1-3: Portrait of the righteous
> 4-6: Portrait of the godless

c. Interpretation

Verse 1 is an *ashre* formula, which exclaims an expressive wonder, an intensity of feeling: "Happy are those . . ." Beatitudes or *macarisms* were common in Egypt and Mesopotamia. So here the psalmist follows a well-established literary tradition of the ancient Orient. The life of a righteous person is described in a negative fashion with the help of three verbs denoting bodily postures/movements: "do not *follow* the advice of the wicked or *take* the path of sinners" (continuing, persisting enduring in sin) and "*sit* in the seat of scoffers" (continue in the company of the insolent). "Advice" is practical wisdom or counsel. "Wicked" are those guilty of sin against God or humans and deserving punishment. "Path" is the mode of life. "Sinners" are human beings who go astray or wander away from Yahweh. "Seat of scoffers" stands for the company of scoffers who are proud or haughty.

Verse 2 is an antithesis of v. 1. "Delight" stands for eagerness and pleasure. "Meditate" means musing or repeating in a low, inaudible voice. "Law" (*Torah*) is the direction and instruction of the priest (Hos. 4:6), prophet (Isa. 42:21, 24), and Yahweh (Jer. 31:33). The righteous are like trees planted by streams of water (Ps. 1:3). "They prosper": they manifest optimism and confidence in God. This is in the context of retribution on earth (Ps. 37:25).

The tragic fate of the impious is demonstrated in v. 4. "Not so": they do not prosper. They are like the chaff that the wind drives away (Ps. 37:36). God will surely punish the wicked. "Judgment" (Ps. 1:5) is not referring to the last judgment but to the assembly in the temple, where the pious offer cult to Yahweh. Here God exercises his judgment. "Congregation of the righteous" is where there is human sharing in God's free gift of salvation. The sinners are excluded from it. Verse 6 is a confession of faith. The Lord "watches over" is a salvific action.

d. Christian Transposition

The fulfillment of God's salvific will is the surest way of salvation for the believer. His Torah is given to us (cf. Rom. 8:2.4). The Christians are under the law of the Lord. The fulfillment of it is a program of life. In such a case, whatever one does will prosper. There can be a tension between God's will and human free will. A consequence of it can be suffering. Such a person can find a way out by looking at the cross, which leads to the resurrection. Sorrow and joy can be the message of Psalm 1.

ii. Ps. 37: Exhortation to Patience and Trust

1   Do not fret because of the wicked;
    do not be envious of wrongdoers.

2   For they will soon fade like the grass.
    and wither like the green herb.

3   Trust in the LORD, and do good
    so you will live in the land and enjoy security.

4   Take delight in the LORD
    and he will give you the desires of your heart.

5   Commit your way to the LORD;
    trust in him, and he will act.

6   He will make your vindication shine like the light
    and the justice of your cause like the noonday.

7   Be still before the LORD, and wait patiently for him;
    do not fret over those who prosper in their way,
    over those who carry out evil devices.

8 Refrain from anger, and forsake wrath,
   do not fret—it leads only to evil.

9 For the wicked shall be cut off,
   but those who wait for the LORD shall inherit the land.

10 Yet a little while, and the wicked will be no more;
   though you look diligently for their place, they will not
   be there.

11 But the meek shall inherit the land,
   and delight themselves in abundant prosperity.

12 The wicked plot against the righteous,
   and gnash their teeth at them;

13 but the LORD laughs at the wicked,
   for he sees that their day is coming.

14 The wicked draw the sword and bend their bows
   to bring down the poor and needy,
   to kill those who walk uprightly;

15 their sword shall enter their own heart,
   and their bows shall be broken.

16 Better is a little that the righteous person has
   than the abundance of many wicked.

17 For the arms of the wicked shall be broken
   but the LORD upholds the righteous.

18 The LORD knows the days of the blameless,
   and their heritage will abide forever;

19 they are not put to shame in evil times,
    in the days of famine they have abundance.

20 But the wicked perish
    and the enemies of the LORD are like the glory of the pastures;
    they vanish—like smoke they vanish away.

21 The wicked borrow, and do not pay back,
    but the righteous are generous and keep giving;

22 for those blessed by the LORD shall inherit the land
    but those cursed by him shall be cut off.

23 Our steps are made firm by the LORD
    when he delights in our way;

24 though we stumble we shall not fall headlong,
    for the LORD holds us by the hand.

25 I have been young and now am old
    yet I have not seen the righteous forsaken
    or their children begging bread.

26 They are ever giving liberally and lending,
    and their children become a blessing.

27 Depart from evil, and do good;
    so you shall abide forever.

28 For the LORD loves justice;
    he will not forsake his faithful ones.
    The righteous shall be kept safe forever,
    but the children of the wicked shall be cut off.

29 The righteous shall inherit the land and live in it forever.

30 The mouths of the righteous utter wisdom,
    and their tongues speak justice.

31 The law of their God is in their hearts;
    their steps do not slip.

32 The wicked watch for the righteous,
    and seek to kill them.

33 The LORD will not abandon them to their power,
    or let them be condemned when they are brought to trial.

34 Wait for the LORD, and keep to his way,
    and he will exalt you to inherit the land;
    you will look on the destruction of the wicked.

35 I have seen the wicked oppressing,
    and towering like a cedar of Lebanon.

36 Again I passed by, and they were no more;
    though I sought them, they could not be found.

37 Mark the blameless, and behold the upright,
    for there is posterity for the peaceable.

38 But transgressors shall be altogether destroyed;
    the posterity of the wicked shall be cut off.

39 The salvation of the righteous is from the LORD,
    he is their refuge in the time of trouble.

40 The LORD helps them and rescues them,
    he rescues them from the wicked, and saves them,
    because they take refuge in him.

a. Introduction

The theme of Ps. 37 is retribution, trying to contrast the lot of the righteous and the wicked. It tries to give an answer to the good fortune of the wicked. Ps. 37 is sapiential in tone, style, and theme. The sapiential style lies in the taste for simple antithesis (Ps. 37:9); in the alteration between enunciations and counsel (Ps. 37:8, 9); in the frequency of motivations (Ps. 37:24, 28); in the reference to experience (Ps. 37:25, 35). It is an acrostic psalm.

b. Structure

This is an anthology of proverbial material.

c. Interpretation

There are two frequent phrases in the psalm: "the righteous inherit the land" (Ps. 37:9, 11, 22, 29, 34) and "the wicked cut off" (Ps. 37:9, 22, 28b, 34, 38). "The righteous" and "the wicked" (Ps. 37:12, 16, 17, 21, 28-29, 38-40) signify not only good and bad, just and wicked, upright and ungodly, but also innocent and guilty.

They (the righteous) shall inherit the land. The fundamental deliverance, exodus, is articulated in three moments: a) coming out of Egypt, from slavery; b) passing through the desert, overcoming the trials; c) entering the land to take possession of it. In the third stage, the liberation is complete. God's plan, however, is frustrated. The righteous are robbed of their land. Here comes the action of the wicked alluded to in the psalm. It is their injustice and oppression that make them enemies of the Lord, who puts himself on the side of the innocent oppressed

(Isa. 1:40). The psalm confronts a social problem, which is also religious.

The wicked triumphs through cunning, a plot against the just. Such a person seeks to put down the poor and the lowly. What ought to be the reaction of the innocent, the righteous, against these machinations? They are to try to restrain them (Ps. 37:1, 7, 8) and then do good (Ps. 37:3). They are not to have recourse to violence. The *anawim* must keep themselves to be *saddiqim*.

Because of the action of God, the oppressed and dispossessed can in some way go through the fundamental process of liberation; a) come out from (Ps. 37:6, 40); b) pass through (walk along) the way of the Lord (Ps. 37:34, 23); c) inherit the land (Ps. 37:3, 11, 29). Thus the original plan of God will be re-established. The author makes a theoretical reflection on a social and religious problem and seeks for an answer reflecting on the date of the history of salvation.

iii. Ps. 73: Plea for Relief from Oppressors

1   Truly God is good to the upright;
    to those who are pure in heart.

2   But as for me, my feet had almost stumbled;
    my steps had nearly slipped.

3   For I was envious of the arrogant;
    I saw the prosperity of the wicked.

4   For they have no pain;
    their bodies are sound and sleek.

5   They are not in trouble as others are;
    they are not plagued like other people.

6   Therefore pride is their necklace;
    violence covers them like a garment.

7   Their eyes swell out with fatness;
    their hearts overflow with follies.

8   They scoff and speak with malice;
    loftily they threaten oppression.

9   They set their mouths against heaven,
    and their tongues range over the earth.

10 Therefore the people turn and praise them,
    and find no fault in them.

11 And they say, "How can God know?
    Is there knowledge in the Most High?"

12 Such are the wicked;
    always at ease, they increase in riches.

13 All in vain I have kept my heart clean
    and washed my hands in innocence.

14 For all day long I have been plagued
    and am punished every morning.

15 If I had said, "I will talk on in this way,"
    I would have been untrue to the circle of your children.

16 But when I thought how to understand this,
    it seemed to me a wearisome task,

17 until I went into the sanctuary of God;
    then I perceived their end.

18 Truly you set them in slippery places;
    you make them fall to ruin.

19 How they are destroyed in a moment,
    swept away utterly by terrors!

20 They are like a dream when one awakes;
    on awakening you despise their phantoms.

21 When my soul was embittered,
    when I was pricked in heart,

22 I was stupid and ignorant;
    I was like a brute beast toward you.

23 Nevertheless I am continually with you;
    you hold my right hand.

24 You guide me with your counsel,
    and afterward you will receive me with honor.

25 Whom have I in heaven but you?
    And there is nothing on earth that I desire other than you.

26 My flesh and my heart may fail,
    but God is the strength of my heart and my portion forever.

27 Indeed, those who are far from you will perish;
    you put an end to those who are false to you.

28 But for me it is good to be near God;
    I have made the Lord God my refuge,
    to tell of all your works.

a. Introduction

Ps. 73 occupies a foremost place among the more mature fruits borne by the struggles through which the OT faith had to pass. It is a powerful testimony to a battle fought in a human soul, comparable with the Book of Job. This psalm carries within it the most profound insights in this regard. In fact, it is unsurpassed in the OT. Ps. 73 is a human confession whereby the psalmist reveals his struggle for a loving communion of faith with his God, a struggle that brought him to the verge of despair.

b. Structure

> 73:1-2: Statement of the principle of retribution
> 3-14: Offence taken at the prosperity of the wicked
> 15-20: New light as regards the wicked
> 21-26: New light as regards his relation to God
> 27-28: Statement of the principle

c. Interpretation

Ps. 73:1-14: Jealousy Aroused by the Prosperity of the Wicked

Ps. 73 is the composition of a pious person who compares his lot with that of the wicked. That person is led to a revelation (v. 17) that shows him the fate of the wicked and the continuing support for him from God.

The question of the beginning is, "How can one maintain one's faith, when the wicked prosper?" There is statement of principle in v. 1 (cf. vv. 27-28), which is the foundation to which one clings in defiance of all his doubts. But there is a struggle in that person: Is there any sense in holding on to belief in God? This is expressed in v. 2, which contains a situation of despair (cf. vv. 13-14).

The jealousy aroused by the prosperity of the wicked is seen in Ps. 73:3-5. One is more indignant at the behaviour and success of the wicked. They display pride and violence like jewelry and garments (Ps. 73:6). The author sarcastically describes their prosperity and their guilt (Ps. 73:7-8). The question underlying it is, Is there a living God? Their slanderous tongue stops at nothing (Ps. 73:9). They are the center of the world (Ps. 73:10). They ask, How come God does not care for the conduct and welfare of his people (Ps. 73:11)? These wicked people are always lucky and accumulate riches (Ps. 73:12). When these things are allowed to happen, where is God? Consequently, there is mental distress and inward tension in the sufferer (Ps. 73:13-14).

Ps. 73:15-28: Enlightenment from Faith

The pivotal part of the psalm is vv. 15-17. The psalmist has not yet renounced his relationship to God; his loyalty to the community has kept him from doing so (Ps. 73:15). Even doubt about God does not help him to find a solution until his faith was renewed when he went into the sanctuary (Ps. 73:17). This was an experience in the temple and in the temple school of wisdom. Now the prosperity of the wicked is seen in a different light (Ps. 73:18-22). He perceives their end (Ps. 73:17). Their outward appearance is not the final thing, as their security is not based on a firm foundation (Ps. 73:18). Their assured happiness collapses (Ps. 73:19). Their life is like a dream (Ps. 73:20). He revalues all his former values. The invisible reality of God becomes, by faith, the unshakable foundation of seeing and thinking. Earlier, the psalmist was like a brute beast toward God (Ps. 73:21-22). There was a materialistic and superficial quality in his former attitude, a fundamental difference between human and divine ways of thinking.

In verse 23, "nevertheless" is an indication of faith. The author speaks as one who does not see and yet believes. God will sustain him, even when he is unable to walk by himself. The humility of the believer is expressed in v. 24. The mystery still remains. There is reference here of a life after death. There is a joy in the present life of union with God (Ps. 73:25). Verse 26 is a reference to the conquering of suffering through faith. One's suffering is not abolished but continues. It is, however, endured thanks to the power of faith. Verses 27-28 make a statement of the principle of retribution.

V. PSALMS OF TRUST
(SONGS OF CONFIDENCE)

A hymn is liturgical. A song is non-liturgical. The cry of an individual or community implies a confidence or hope that there is someone capable of overcoming the threat (death or chaos threatening order). This is the reason why a lament can become a prayer.

There is in the laments an element that Gunkel called "the certainty of hearing." This certainty is usually expressed at the end of the lament (Ps. 13:5, 5:12, 6:9-10, 57:10, 58:17, 62:12). This element became the core of some songs (Ps. 23:27). In the songs of confidence, the idea of security (Ps. 4:8, 16:8-9, 27:1-5) and of peace, even during sleep (Ps. 16:9), is frequently mentioned. The thought of trust provides joy (Ps. 16:6, 9, 11; 23:6). In these psalms, the personal tone is more apparent than in thanksgiving psalms.

i.   Ps. 23: The Lord: Shepherd and Host

1   The LORD is my shepherd, I shall not want.

2   He makes me lie down in green pastures;
    he leads me beside still waters;

3   he restores my soul.
    He leads me in right paths,
    for his name's sake.

4   Even though I walk through the darkest valley,
    I fear no evil;
    for you are with me;
    your rod and your staff—
    they comfort me.

5 You prepare a table before me
in the presence of my enemies;
you anoint my head with oil;
my cup overflows.

6 Surely goodness and mercy shall follow me
all the days of my life,
and I shall dwell in the house of the LORD
my whole life long.

a. Introduction

Ps. 23 is one of the most loved psalms in tradition, in the liturgy, in private prayer, in music, and in art. The theme of the shepherd (pastor) is linked to the tradition of David, the shepherd, and in the church to the task of the leaders of the church.

The pastoral scene is the object of the genius of poets, artists, and musicians (Beethoven, Berlioz, Honegger).

The two characteristics of the psalm are simplicity and richness. It is simple in its construction and development, made with sober strokes of the brush. Its wealth lies in the incredible repertoire of symbols.

This psalm seems to revolve around the title: the Lord shepherd (Ps. 23:1) However, the pastoral scene seems to change about the middle of the psalm (Ps. 23:5). So we have two images: the Lord is shepherd and host.

b. Structure

23:1-4: The Lord is shepherd
5-6: The Lord is host

c. Interpretation

23:1-4: The Lord Is My Shepherd

In the OT, the shepherd can represent a leader (David) and God (Exodus: Yahweh as the shepherd of his people in the desert). The image of shepherd is found in the relationship between a person and an animal. It can be a relationship of hostility (defence and hunting) or friendship and dominion (defending one's sheep, going in search of the lost). Applying the same image of God, people can humanise their beastly tendencies and offer themselves as domesticated to the guidance of God. This is a generic value diffused throughout the psalm.

The image of the shepherd is developed with realism and conciseness in a series of small scenes. The author does not give minute descriptions but captures a privileged moment; he records it and moves on. One touch of his brush is able to evoke a whole scene: a green pasture with a fountain meant for resting, lying down, restoration of breath and energies, leading along the right path in an obscure valley with the rod and staff. Poetry works with words "to frame the human condition, to freeze it for ever" (Allan Kirschner).

The first verse is a clue that the rest of the psalm should be read as imagery. The author is not speaking of sheep only, but of himself as one sheep in a flock. So there are two levels of meaning. Everything is said of sheep, and yet "soul," "right paths," "name," and "restores" are ambiguous. "For you are with me" (Ps. 23:4) is an intensely personal expression.

23:5-6: The Lord Is the Host

Hospitality (cf. Gen. 18:1-18) is important; in Asian cultures, it is considered a right. Once hospitality is extended, the guest is sacred and must be defended against enemies, even to the extent of harm to one's family. A spiritual dimension is superimposed on it: "goodness," "mercy," "the house of the Lord" (Ps. 23:6). Goodness and mercy belong to God. "Anoint" (Ps. 23:5) is a gesture of hospitality.

The whole psalm has a movement to the last verse. One will live to the end of one's life in the house of the Lord. It is not only as his guest but indeed as a member of his household (i.e., the most intimate and unbroken fellowship with God). The main emphasis is not on the external nearness to the temple but on the spiritual aspect of his communion with God.

What unites the roles of shepherd and host is the Lord's role in the exodus (water, food, rest), in the Promised Land where he as the host receives them (Ps. 68:10, 77:20; Ex. 15:13), and in the temple.

d. Christian Transposition

Jn 10:1-18 portrays Christ as the true shepherd (Jn 10:11). 1 Pet. 2:25 says, "You who were straying like sheep have returned to the shepherd and guardian of your souls." 1 Pet. 5:2-4 speaks of tending the flock willingly and eagerly. The symbolism of the psalm can be extended to the church, which is the fundamental sacrament, in which there is an image of the flock in movement until it reaches the Father's house. The sacraments are their comfort, which comes to them through the water of revivification, the bread and the cup of the Eucharist, and the anointing. Ps. 23 is a sacramental psalm. "The symbol makes one think" (Ricoeur). The symbols in the psalm makes one think much.

ii.   Ps. 121: God, the Keeper

1   I lift up my eyes to the hills—
     from where will my help come?

2   My help comes from the LORD,
     who made heaven and earth.

3   He will not let your foot be moved;
     he who keeps you will not slumber.

4   He who keeps Israel
     will neither slumber nor sleep.

5   The LORD is your keeper,
     the LORD is your shade at your right hand.

6   The sun shall not strike you by day,
     nor the moon by night.

7   The LORD will keep you from all evil;
     he will keep your life.

8   The LORD will keep
     your going out and your coming in
     from this time on and forevermore.

a.   Introduction

Ps. 121 is a song of ascents. In it, there is the development of one idea in a concise way.

b. Structure

121:1: Question
2-8: Answer

c. Interpretation

The psalm is a kind of anonymous dialogue: Ps. 121:1-2 and 3-8 (the supplicant addressed in the second person). The eyes are lifted up to the hills (v. 1). The gaze is charged with a question, and it receives an answer that is coming from another voice, which may be from the inner self of the supplicant. The frequent repetition of "you" implies the creator taking particular care of one individual. The Lord is his keeper (Ps. 121:5), guardian, custodian. His vigilance over the supplicant is stressed in v. 3: He will not let your foot be moved; he will not slumber. He will neither slumber nor sleep (Ps. 121:4). All can sleep because the Lord does not sleep.

He will defend Israel from every evil. This totality is expressed through polarity: sun and moon (day and night; i.e., all time), going out and coming in (all the activity; life), this time forth and forever more (now and forever) (Deut. 28:6, 1 Kgs 3:7).

The ending of the psalm is still open for further development. Knowing that the mother is vigilant, the child can close his eyes and sleep peacefully in spite of the "going" and "coming" of the cradle. In our lives, too, we raise our eyes anxiously to God and see his presence (vigilant presence), and we become calm. This can take place even at the last closing of our eyes, because our keeper does not slumber.

d. Christian Transposition

In Jn 17:12: "While I was with them, I protected them in your name that you have given me." 2 Thess. 3:3: "The Lord is faithful; he will strengthen you and guard you from evil." 1 Pet. 1:5: "Who by God's power are guarded through faith for a salvation ready to be revealed in the last time."

Appendix I

READING PLAN FOR PSALMS

JANUARY		FEBRUARY		MARCH	
1	Ps. 8; 19	1	Ps. 41; 42	1	Ps. 78
2	Ps. 29; 33	2	Ps. 45; 51	2	Ps. 46; 48
3	Ps. 92; 100	3	Ps. 52; 53	3	Ps. 76; 87
4	Ps. 104; 111	4	Ps. 54; 55	4	Ps. 15; 24
5	Ps. 113; 114	5	Ps. 56; 57	5	Ps. 50; 81
6	Ps. 117; 135	6	Ps. 58; 59	6	Ps. 84; 95
7	Ps. 136	7	Ps. 61; 64	7	Ps. 105; 122
8	Ps. 145; 146	8	Ps. 69; 71	8	Ps. 4; 11
9	Ps. 147; 148	9	Ps. 77; 86	9	Ps. 16; 23
10	Ps. 149; 150	10	Ps. 88; 89	10	Ps. 27; 62
11	Ps. 9; 18	11	Ps. 94; 102	11	Ps. 63; 91
12	Ps. 30; 32	12	Ps. 109; 120	12	Ps. 121; 131
13	Ps. 34; 40	13	Ps. 130; 139	13	Ps. 1; 37
14	Ps. 41; 103	14	Ps. 140; 141	14	Ps. 49
15	Ps. 66	15	Ps. 142; 143	15	Ps. 73
16	Ps. 116; 118	16	Ps. 144; 68	16	Ps. 112
17	Ps. 65; 67	17	Ps. 44; 60	17	Ps. 119:1-40
18	Ps. 75; 107	18	Ps. 74; 79	18	Ps. 119:41-80
19	Ps. 124; 126	19	Ps. 80; 83	19	Ps. 119:81-120
20	Ps. 134; 138	20	Ps. 85; 90	20	Ps. 119:121-160
21	Ps. 3; 4	21	Ps. 115; 123	21	Ps. 119:161-176
22	Ps. 5; 6	22	Ps. 125; 129	22	Ps. 127; 128
23	Ps. 7; 10	23	Ps. 137; 82	23	Ps. 106; 133

JANUARY	FEBRUARY	MARCH
24 Ps. 12; 13	24 Ps. 47; 93	24 Ps. 139
25 Ps. 14; 17	25 Ps. 95; 96	25 Ps. 72; 110
26 Ps. 22; 25	26 Ps. 97; 98	26 Ps. 132.
27 Ps. 26; 27	27 Ps. 99; 101	
28 Ps. 28; 31	28 Ps. 2; 20	
29 Ps. 35; 36		
30 Ps. 38; 39		
31 Ps. 21; 45		

Appendix II

EXPLORATION OF THE PSALMS

The more we explore and ponder the psalms, the more they will deepen our relationship with God. There is a six-step strategy for getting acquainted with a psalm:

Step 1. Pray the psalm aloud.

Step 2. Give the psalm a careful second reading. Ask some simple questions to establish clearly in your own mind what is going on in the psalm.

Step 3. Look for lines you could easily make a part of your prayers. Ask yourself, what do I like about this psalm? What do I resonate to? Could any of these lines help me express myself to God?

Step 4. Explore the unfamiliar or puzzling parts of the psalm. The parts of the psalms that are strange to us usually have the greatest potential for teaching us. But in order to understand what is strange or confusing, we must put some effort into learning.

Step 5. Ask how the psalm applies to you. Now that you have examined how the psalmist prays, compare his way of praying to your own.

Step 6. Pray the psalm again. Praying the psalm is not a onetime step. The goal of working your way through a psalm is to add something to your ongoing conversation with God. So give the psalm a chance to do this. Pray the psalm over and over. Pray it with feeling. The more you pray it, the more you will see in it, and the greater the effect it will have on you.[291]

---

[291] Perrotta, *Psalms*.

Appendix III

PRAYING THE PSALMS

Sunday: Morning Prayer Ps. 29 and Ps. 92
             Evening Prayer Ps. 9 and Ps. 103

Monday: Morning Prayer Ps. 4 and Ps. 11
             Evening Prayer Ps. 2 and Ps. 20

Tuesday: Morning Prayer Ps. 135 and Ps. 145
             Evening Prayer Ps. 91 and Ps. 131

Wednesday: Morning Prayer Ps. 44 and Ps. 60
             Evening Prayer Ps. 10 and Ps. 12

Thursday: Morning Prayer Ps. 24 and Ps. 50
             Evening Prayer Ps. 26 and Ps. 27

Friday: Morning Prayer Ps. 61 and Ps. 64
             Evening Prayer Ps. 77 and Ps. 88

Saturday: Morning Prayer Ps. 65 and Ps. 67
             Evening Prayer Ps. 128 and Ps. 133

2. Advent Season: Morning Prayer Ps. 38 and Ps. 120
             Evening Prayer Ps. 19 and Ps. 111

3. Christmas Season: Morning Prayer Ps. 117 and Ps. 147
             Evening Prayer Ps. 148 and Ps. 150

4. Lenten Season: Morning Prayer Ps. 74 and Ps. 130
Evening Prayer Ps. 3 and Ps. 90

5. Easter Season: Morning Prayer Ps. 63 and Ps. 23
Evening Prayer Ps. 95 and Ps. 13

Appendix IV

GLOSSARY OF TERMS

Anointing (Anoint, Anointed, Anointment)

Objects or persons could receive a sacred anointing. The kings and high priests who receive sacred anointing were solemnly consecrated as an initiation into their sacred office. Anointing of kings is the normal, outward sign of their divine election to the kingship. The king remains as "the anointed of Yahweh." The actual anointing is performed by a prophet as Yahweh's representative or by the high priest together with a prophet. It endows the recipient with preternatural power and authority, whereby he shares in Yahweh's own powerful life. The sacred anointing took place at some holy site.

Ark

The ark of Noah was made of cypress wood and coated inside and out with pitch to make it watertight. The ark of infant Moses was a papyrus basket made watertight with bitumen and pitch. The ark of the covenant of the Lord (Numbers 10:33) was one of the principal objects of the tabernacle and was kept in the Most Holy Place. The ark was an oblong gold-covered acacia chest lined with gold. It measured 2.5 cubits by 1.5 cubits by 1.5 cubits. The two stone tablets on which the Decalogue was inscribed (Exodus 25:16, Deuteronomy 10:1-5), a golden pot containing manna and the rod of Aaron (Hebrews 9:4), and a copy of the Mosaic Law (Deuteronomy 31:25-26) were kept inside the ark.

The ark was a sort of war-palladium, a sacred object, which was carried into battle and the sight of which threw Israel's enemies into panic.

David

David was an Ephraimite of Bethlehem of Judah, the youngest son of Jesse. He founded the independent kingdom of United Israel. David is the greatest king of Israel. He composed some psalms. The Messiah is a descendant of David.

Faithfulness (*emet*)

An attribute of God (Exodus 34:6) directed towards the people of the covenant. It is a free gift and a term of the covenant. God's fidelity is seen to be steady throughout the history of salvation. The name symbolises God's unchangeable fidelity.

Fear of the Lord

It is not a psychological fear, but one based essentially on the feeling of reverence and awe for God. The stress is on what God is rather than on what he might do. Fear of the Lord is tantamount to religious piety and divine worship (Deuteronomy 10:12). It is the beginning of wisdom.

Feasts

The Israelites (Jewish people) had many feasts. Their festivals were classified as weekly, monthly, annual, cyclic, and post-exilic:

1) The weekly and monthly festivals were the sabbath and the new moon. The new moon marked the beginning of the new month based on astronomical observations.

2) The annual festivals were **Passover, Pentecost, Tabernacles, Day of Atonement,** and **New Year's Day.** **Passover** commemorates the deliverance (passing over) from Egypt. **Pentecost** is the Greek term (meaning "fiftieth day") for the Jewish Feast of Weeks. From the second day of the Passover week, seven weeks were counted, and Pentecost was celebrated the next day. It marked the beginning of free will offerings of first fruits. The **Feast of the Tabernacles** happened in the month of Tishri. It lasted one week, during which the people had to dwell in tents or booths erected in the streets and open spaces. It was to remind the Israelites of the time when their ancestors lived in tents after their departure from Egypt. The **Day of Atonement** is the annual day of fasting and expiation for the sins of the nation, when the high priest offered sacrifices as atonement for himself, the priesthood, and all the people. **New Year's Day** remembers the religious year, regulating the annual cycle of festivals with the first of the month of Nisan (March/April) in the spring.

3) The cyclic festivals are the **Sabbatical Year** and **Year of the Jubilee.** The Sabbatical Year meant a year's rest for the land, a year during which no debtor could be forced to pay his debt, and a year for the reading of the law. The Jubilee Year, the fiftieth year, occurred after 7 times 7 years, or 49 years. The whole land rested. All landed property reverted to the original owners or to their descendants without payment. All Israelites who had been reduced to slavery were set at liberty.

4) Post-exilic festivals were the **Feast of Purim** and **Feast of the Dedication of the Temple.** The Feast of Purim (lots) recalls the plan to kill the Jews by the Persian governor, Amman, frustrated through Queen Esther. It is celebrated on the 14th and 15th of Adar, observing the 13th as a fast day. The feast was celebrated by reading the Book of Esther aloud in the synagogues; joyous

feasts were held in the houses. Feast of the Dedication of the Temple was kept every year on the 25th day of Kislev (Nov./Dec.) to commemorate the purification of the temple from idolatrous worship of Antiochus IV Epiphanes, and its dedication by Judas Maccabeus.

God: His Names

Judaism has many names for God. He is named *Yahweh* (Lord), *Elohim* (God), *El* (the strong one, God), *Elyon* (Highest, Most High), *Shadday* (Almighty), and so on. *Yahweh* (Lord) is the proper name of the God of Israel. He is considered the king. The kings on earth are representatives of the Kingship of God. Jesus, the Messiah (Saviour), is also a King.

Judaism

The total way of life of the Israelite (Jewish) community is Judaism. They were the chosen people of God, descendants from Abraham, the chosen one. They have a covenantal relationship with God. All the Israelites acknowledge the *Torah* (law). Since they all sinned, they were waiting for the coming of the Messiah, who would liberate them from their sins. Christ, the Messiah, came. His followers, the Christians, formed Christianity. Consequently Christianity can be seen as a sort of evolution of Judaism.

Pharisees

A religious party that sought the perfect expression of spiritual life through the strict observance of the law alone. A Pharisee is one who "separates himself."

Rabbi (Master)

An honourary and respectful title used by Jewish students for their teachers.

Righteous, Righteousness

Right conduct, as opposed to sin, wickedness, and so on. It is honesty as opposed to deception, truthfulness as opposed to lying (Gen. 30:33). The *righteous* is the person who serves God (Mal. 3:18) and lives by his fidelity. *Righteousness* saves one from death (Prov. 10:2); life is found in its path (Prov. 12:28); it wins a crown (Prov. 16:31).

Retribution

Retribution is a reward granted by God to the just or punishment inflicted by him on the sinner.

Sacrifices

An Old Testament sacrifice was an offering of a gift to God, making the gift a victim in place of oneself to acknowledge God's absolute majesty. In this, a person was giving a portion of one's personal goods to God. A sacrifice was thus a reminder of people's humble dependence on God. These sacrifices could be bloody or unbloody. Bloody sacrifices could be of animals or doves (human sacrifices were forbidden). The unbloody sacrifices could be of grain, wine, oil, salt, or incense. The Old Testament sacrifices were only examples of the one true sacrifice, the sacrificial death of Christ on the cross of Calvary. Christ, the Messiah, gave himself as the ultimate sacrifice, abolishing all the Old Testament sacrifices.

Steadfast Love

Steadfast love is one of the conditions of the covenant between Yahweh and the chosen people of God. God's steadfast love is an unfailing love. An act of such love is forgiveness from God. It is also associated with the relationship with the people. Steadfast love serves as a summary of Israel's understanding of the character of God.

BIBLIOGRAPHY

Allen, Leslie C. *Word Biblical Themes: Psalms*. Waco, TX: Word Books, 1987.

Allen, Leslie C. *Psalms 101-150, Word Biblical Commentary, 21*. Edited by David A. Hubbard et al. Waco, TX: Word Books, 1983.

Atherton, Richard. *New Light*. Mumbai: Pauline Publications, 1996.

Anderson, A. A. *The Book of Psalms*. Vol. 1, *Psalms 1-72. The New Century Bible*. London: Oliphants, 1981.

Barclay, W. "Psalm 8: God and Man," in *The Lord Is My Shepherd: Expositions of Selected Psalms*. Glasgow, Scotland: William Collins, 1982.

Berlin, Adele. "Introduction to the Hebrew Poetry," in *New Interpreter's Bible*. Vol. 4. Edited by L. E. Keck. Nashville, TN: Abingdon Press, 1996.

Briggs, C. A., and E. G. Briggs. *The Book of Psalms. The International Critical Commentary*. Edited by S. R. Driver et al. Edinburgh: T. & T. Clark, 1969.

Brook, John. *The School of Prayer. An Introduction to the Divine Office for All Christians*. London: Harper Collins, 1992.

Brown, Raymond E., et al. *The New Jerome Biblical Commentary*. Bangalore: Theological Publications in India (TPI), 1990.

Brueggemann, Walter. *The Message of the Psalms. A Theological Commentary*. Augsburg Old Testament Studies. Minneapolis: Augsburg, 1984.

Brueggemann, Walter. *Praying the Psalms*. Winona, MN: St. Mary's Press, 1986.

Brueggemann, Walter. *Spirituality of the Psalms*. Minneapolis: Fortress Press, 2002.

Canham, Elizabeth. *Praying the Bible.* London: The Bible Reading Fellowship, 1988.

Castelliono, G. *Libro Dei Salmi.* Torino, 1955.

Chittister, Joan D. *Songs of Joy. New Meditations on the Psalms for Every Day of the Year.* New York: Crossroad Publishing, 1997.

Coughlan, P. "Praising God in the Psalms." *Clergy Review* 63 (1978), 369-375, 465-475; 64 (1979), 92-96.

Craghan, John F. *Psalms for All Seasons.* Bangalore: IJA Publications, 1996.

Craigie, Peter C. *Psalms 1-50.* Edited by D. A. Hubbard and G. W. Barker. *Word Biblical Commentary 19.* Waco: Word, 1983.

Creach, Jerome F. D. *Psalms: Interpretations.* Bible Studies. Louisville, KY: Westminster John Knox Press, 1998.

Crenshaw, James L. *The Psalms. An Introduction.* Grand Rapids, MI: Eerdmans, 2001.

Dahood, M. *Psalms I: 1-50.* The Anchor Bible. Garden City, NY: Doubleday, 1965.

Delitzsch, F. *Psalms,* Vol. 5 in *Commentary on the Old Testament.* Edited by C. F Keil and F. Delitzsch. Book 3. Grand Rapids, MI: Eerdmans, 1980.

Drijivers, P. *The Psalms: Their Structure and Meaning.* Freiburg: Herder, 1965.

Eaton, J. H. "The Psalms and Israelite Worship", in *Tradition and Interpretation,* edited by G. W. Anderson, Engel I. *Critical Essays on the Old Testament,* London, 1970.

Engnell, I. *Critical Essays on the Old Testament.* London, 1970.

Estes, Daniel J. *Handbook on the Wisdom Books and Psalms.* Grand Rapids, MI: Baker Academic, 2005.

Farmer, Kathleen. "Psalms 42-89." In *The International Bible Commentary. An Ecumenical Commentary for Twenty-First Century,* edited by William R. Farmer. Bangalore: TPI, 2004.

Farmer, William R., et al., eds. *The International Bible Commentary.* Bangalore: TPT, 2004.

Farnes, Pedro S. *Praying the Psalms. Introducing the Psalms for Morning and Evening Prayers.* Bangalore: Claretian Publications, 1995.

Geissler, Eugene S., ed. *The Bible Prayer Book.* Notre Dame, IN: Ave Maria Press, 1981.

Gelin, Albert. *The Psalms Are Our Prayers.* Collegeville, MN: Liturgical Press, 1964.

Gerstenberger, Erhard S. *Psalms. Part 1 with an Introduction to Cultic Poetry.* Volume XIV of *The Forms of the Old Testament Literature.* Grand Rapids, MI: Eerdmans, 1988.

Gerstenberger, Erhard S. "Psalms," in *OT Form Criticism,* edited by J. H. Hayes. San Antonio, TX: Trinity University Press, 1974.

Gottwald, N. K. "Poetry, Hebrew," *IDB III,* 829-838.

Gunkel, H. *The Psalms. A Form-Critical Introduction.* Philadelphia: Fortress, 1967.

Hayes, J. H. *An Introduction to Old Testament Study.* Nashville, TN: Abingdon, 1979.

Hempel, J. "Psalms, Book of," *IDB III,* 942-958.

Hillers, D. R. "A Study of Psalm 148," CBQ 40 (1978), 323-334.

Iglesias, Yolanda, and Salvatore. *The Promise. An Introduction to the Old Testament.* Makati City: Word and Life Publications, 1996.

Johnson, A. R. "The Psalms," in *The OT and Modern Study.* Edited by H. H. Rowley. London: Oxford University Press, 1974, 179-224.

Juengling, Hans-Winfried. "Psalms 1-41," in *The International Bible Commentary. An Ecumenical Commentary for Twenty-First Century,* edited by William R. Farmer. Bangalore: TPI, 2004.

Kaempchen, Martin. *The Holy Waters.* Indian Psalm Meditations. Bangalore: ATC, 1995.

Keck, Leander E., et al. *The New Interpreter's Bible.* Vol. 4. Nashville, TN: Abingdon Press, 1996.

Kinder, Derek. *Psalms 1-72. An Introduction and Commentary on the Books I and II of the Psalms.* Tyndale OT Commentaries. Leicester, UK: Inter-Varsity Press, 1973.

Kinder, Derek. *Psalms 73-150. A Commentary on Books III, IV, and V of the Psalms.* Tyndale OT Commentaries. Leicester, UK: Inter-Varsity Press, 1975.

Knight, George A. F. *Psalms. Volume 1.* The Daily Study Bible Series. Philadelphia: Westminster Press, 1983.

Knight, George A. F. *Psalms. Volume 2.* The Daily Study Bible Series. Philadelphia: Westminster Press, 1983.

Kodel, J. "The Poetry of the Psalms," *BT* 65 (1973), 1107-1113.

Kraus, Hans-Joachim. *Psalms 1-59. A Commentary.* Translated by Hilton C. Oswald. Minneapolis: Augsburg Publishing House, 1988.

Kraus, Hans-Joachim. *Theology of the Psalms.* Translated by Keith Crim. Minneapolis: Augsburg Publishing House, 1986.

Kselman, J. S., and M. L. Barré. "Psalms," in *NJBC.* Edited by R. E. Brown, et al. Bangalore: TPI, 1991, pp. 523-552.

Lewis, C. S. *Reflections on the Psalms.* Collins: Fount Paperbacks, 1961.

Luke, K. *Israel Before Yahweh: An Exposition of Selected Psalms.* Quilon: Assisi Press, 1978.

Luke, K. *Taste and See. Aids to the Fruitful Recitation of the Breviary.* Cochin: Impress, 1980.

Martin, Francis. *Songs of God's People: The Psalms as Poetry and Prayer.* Denville: Dimension Books, 1978.

Martini, Carlo Maria. *What Am I That You Care For Me? Praying with the Psalms.* Collegeville, MN: Liturgical Press, 1990.

Mays, A. D. H. "The Psalms and their Use in Worship," *Scripture in Church,* 7 (1976-1977), 88-98.

McCann, "Psalms for Moderns: Picture Prayer," *Sursum Corda* 11 (1970-1971), 15-22.

McCann, J. Clinton Jr. "The Book of Psalms," in *The New Interpreter's Bible,* Vol. 4. Edited by L. E. Keck. Nashville, TN: Abingdon Press, 1996, pp. 666-677.

McKenzie, John L. *Dictionary of the Bible.* Bangalore: ATC, 1984.

Merton, Thomas. *Praying the Psalms.* Collegeville, MN: Liturgical Press, 1956.

Mowinckel, S. *The Psalms in Israel's Worship, I, II.* Translated by D. R. Ap-Thomas. Nashville, TN: Abingdon, 1962.

Murphy, R. E. "Psalms," *JBC* 35: 1-18.

Neale, J. M., and R. F. Littledale. *A Commentary on the Psalms: From Primitive and Medieval Writers.* London: Joseph Masters & Co., 1976.

O'Brien, M. "The Psalms," *Annals* 90(1979) 13-28.

Patrick, D. Miller Jr. *Interpreting the Psalms.* Philadelphia: Fortress Press, 1986.

Perrotta, Kevin. *Psalms. An Invitation to Prayer.* Chicago: Loyola Press, 2000.

Pleins, J. David. *The Psalms. Songs of Tragedy, Hope, and Justice.* Maryknoll, NY: Orbis, 1993.

Ravasi, Gianfranco. "Psalms 90-150." In William R. Framer, *The International Bible Commentary. An Ecumenical Commentary for the Twenty-First Century.* Bangalore: TPI, 204, pp. 898-916.

Rippin, Robert. *Praying the Psalms.* Homebush: St. Paul Publications, 1990.

Rogerson, J. W., and J. W. McKay. *Psalms 1-50.* Cambridge: Cambridge University Press, 1977.

Rogerson, J. W., and J. W. McKay. *Psalms 51-100.* Cambridge: Cambridge University Press, 1977.

Rogerson, J. W., and J. W. McKay. *Psalms 101-150.* Cambridge: Cambridge University Press, 1977.

Rosage, David E. *The Lord Is My Shepherd. Praying the Psalms.* Ann Arbor, MI: Servant Books, 1984.

Sabourin, Leopold. *The Psalms. Their Origin and Meaning.* Bangalore: TPI, 1971.

Schokel, L. A. *Trenta Salmi: Poesia e Preghiera.* Bologna: Dehoniane, 1982.

Shepherd, J. Barrie. *Praying the Psalms. Daily Meditations on Cherished Psalms.* Philadelphia: Westminster Press, 1987.

Stradling, Leslie E. *Praying the Psalms*. Philadelphia: Fortress Press, 1977.

Stuhlmuller, C. *Psalms*. OT Message 21. Wilmington, DE, 1983.

Tate, Marvin E. *Psalms 51-100*. Word Biblical Commentary 20. Dallas: Word Books, 1990.

Terrien, Samuel. *The Psalms*. Grand Rapids, MI: Eerdmans, 2003.

Thekkekara, Mathew V. *The Young in Faith Praying the Psalms Meaningfully*. Bangalore: Asian Trading Corporation, 2005.

Timko, P. "The Psalms: An Introduction to their Historical and Literary Character." *BT* 65 (1973), 1095-1100.

Valles, Carlos G. *Praying Together. Psalms for Contemplation*. Anand: Gujarat Sahitya Prakash, 1994.

Weiser, Artur. *The Psalms*. The Old Testament Library. Translated by Herbert Hartwell. London: SCM Press, 1982.

Westermann, Claus. *Praise and Lament in the Psalms*. Atlanta: John Knox Press, 1981.

Westermann, Claus. *The Psalms. Structure, Content, and Message*. Translated by Ralph D. Gehrke. Minneapolis : Augsburg Publishing House, 1980.

Westermann, Claus. "Book of Psalms," *IDB Sup*. Edited by Keith Crim. Nashville, TN: Abingdon, 1976, pp. 705-710.